I AM A
SUPERHERO
EXPERT

I AM A SUPERHERO EXPERT

Growing up with my Autistic Brother

JOSH STEHLE

Accomplishing
Innovation Press

Accomplishing Innovation Press
1497 Main St. Suite 169
Dunedin, FL 34698
accomplishinginnovationpress.com
AccomplishingInnovationPress@gmail.com

Cover and Typeset by S. Wilder
Edited by Gayle Staggemeyer

Library of Congress Control Number: 2022944617

Paperback ISBN-13: 979-8-8232-0021-9
Hardcover ISBN-13: 979-8-8232-0026-4
Ebook ISBN-13: 979-8-8232-0019-6
Audiobook ISBN-13: 979-8-8232-0028-8

For Zach

TABLE OF CONTENTS

SUPERHEROES

> Who is the lamest superhero? It's got to be Hawkeye, right?
> **Josh**

> That is a good question. I'd go with Marvel's Champions, or DC's Inferior Five.
> **Zach**

> And not Hawkeye? All he's got is a bow and arrow!
> **Josh**

I AM A SUPERHERO EXPERT.

This is deceiving to say, considering I know almost nothing about conventional superheroes, at least when compared to an actual expert.

Sure, I understand the basics. I've read plenty of comic books in my twenty-one years of life, and I've seen almost every superhero movie. I still remember the days in middle school when I would sit in math class and imagine how much cooler my life would have been if I'd had a superpower. It would have been so impressive to stretch my limbs like silly putty and dunk a basketball in 7th grade, and it would have been so much easier to ask my crush to the school dance if I had mesmerizing laser eyes.

I admit, however, that I don't completely understand the intricacies of the Marvel Cinematic Universe, nor have I memorized the DC Universe storylines and their many villains. And, sadly, I probably couldn't name the original seven members of the Justice League, even if Batman held me by my ankles off the side of a building. Honestly, I still confuse the Joker with the Green Goblin on a regular basis. I truly have no conventional superhero expertise.

Nevertheless, despite all that I don't know about superheroes, what I do know is that I, Josh Stehle, *am* a superhero expert.

You see, when it comes to true comic book expertise, my brother, Zach, reigns supreme. He knows everything there is to know about superheroes, from the worlds they live in, to the writers and studios that created them. Stacks of meticulously kept comics surround his bed and climb his bookshelves. In fact, my brother never goes a day without reading his favorite Batman or Spiderman issues, and he always remembers exactly where they reside in his massive comic book collection.

I should mention that Zach is also on the autistic spectrum. Autism, or autism spectrum disorder (ASD), "refers to a broad range of conditions characterized by challenges with social skills, repetitive behavior, speech, and nonverbal communication."[1] These conditions may include anything from the individual having trouble pronouncing words or understanding

---

[1] "AutismSpeaks." https://www.autismspeaks.org/what-autism.

social cues to requiring a strict and consistent daily schedule to be productive. Although common trends and symptoms are shared throughout the autistic spectrum, every individual is different and faces unique obstacles. Autism is not a one-size-fits-all cognitive disorder. It's not like Burger King where you can have it your way. Autism affects every individual differently.

Compared to many people with ASD, Zach's autistic symptoms are mild. He works full-time as a grocery store cashier, has a few close friends, and maintains a perfect credit score. In his free time, he enjoys reading his comic books and watching countless superhero shows on his computer while cuddling with Piper, his pet cat. Piper's cat food and litter box may be the bane of Zach's existence due to his cripplingly weak gag reflex, but he still loves that cat more than life itself and treats her like a queen. Well, that is, except for when he has superheroes on his mind. Then, Piper takes a backseat to the stories of Spiderman, Thor, and Wolverine while Zach disappears into the worlds of Marvel and DC.

Sometimes, I stand in his doorway and watch him as he leans in close to the computer screen in anticipation, ignoring Piper as she walks across his keyboard and paws for his attention.

It's as if nothing else in the world matters except for the superheroes on his screen. His face lights up when they win a close battle, and the dimples on his cheeks reappear. Then, he rewinds the video and watches the battle again.

"Meow!" Perhaps Piper has had enough of Zach's superhero obsession. She butts her head into Zach's stomach, insisting on rubs and pats, which my brother eagerly provides. Then, Zach walks over to his bookshelves, chooses four or five new comics from his massive collection, and, once again, nothing else in the world matters.

Zach is twenty-three. He's my older brother by two years. If you were to see him in public, chances are you wouldn't even know he's on the spectrum. However, unlike *most* twenty-three-year-olds, he has difficulty making decisions that are in what we refer to as a "gray area." Black and white decisions such as where to cross a street, when to wash his hands, and when to brush his teeth are easy for my brother to understand. In fact, Zach thrives in these situations because he knows exactly the rule he needs to follow. But in situations that may require bending a rule or making an exception, the gray area, Zach struggles. Additionally, Zach's speech is not as fluent as it should be. He has trouble remembering the letters of the alphabet and distinguishing left from right. He insists on following every rule and becomes flustered when it isn't possible. He also has difficulty at times expressing interest in topics other than superheroes and fantasy. To many, these challenges would be inhibiting. And to Zach, well, they are, at times. However, I also think that autism has given Zach something extraordinary.

I think that autism has given Zach a superpower.

I wish I could say I was there when Zach cracked open his first comic book, but to be honest, I probably didn't care. After all, I was only nine, the time in my life when I thought the word, "finger," was spelled with a "th" instead of an "f" (It's true, sadly). I was far too young to see the immediate effect that comic books had on him, and I certainly didn't realize the effect that they would have on me until many, many years later. But even at nine, I noticed how his whole demeanor changed when he started to get into comic books, and it didn't take long for that interest to become a passion and for that passion to become an obsession. Ah, yes, obsessions are another common trait for people with ASD.

Marvel's Spiderman was Zach's first love, followed closely by DC's Batman and the Justice League. Zach didn't favor one series or style over any other. He just wanted them all. When the stacks of books started piling around his room, my parents bought cases and bookshelves to house them. As he grew older and his tastes naturally changed, he bought new books to replace the older ones with the money he earned from his job as a grocery store cashier. Through the years, I did my best to contribute to his growing collection, though finding a book he hasn't already read cover to cover is nearly impossible to this day.

I still remember the time I almost gave up on buying Zach comic books forever. It was his birthday week, and I was determined to give him a book he hadn't yet read. On the day before his birthday, I went to the local comic bookstore in town and spent hours raiding the shelves. I put together an epic collection of classic comics, new releases, obscure anime pamphlet things that I didn't even know if he liked or not, and a Green Lantern comic book, because, of course, no one reads Green Lantern comic books, right? By the time I got back home, I couldn't wait to give my brother the gift of all gifts, the bag of books I'd carefully hand-selected and anguished over. He'd be amazed that I knew him so well, and my gift was sure to be better than everybody else's. The next day, I proudly presented him with the collection, only to find out that he had not only read every single one of the books already but also read the Green Lantern comic twice. I was bewildered. He found it amusing.

When Zach learned to drive and got his license, he began leaving the house on his own. At first, my family was concerned for his safety. After all, the world is a dangerous place, and Zach had always been a selfless individual. We were worried somebody would try to take advantage of him or treat him unfairly due to his unique selflessness and genuinely giving personality. However, we learned that the only way for Zach to grow as a person was for him to experience life rather than avoid it. Besides, his insistence on following rules made him a reliable driver, and he was only interested in driving to two places anyway.

Once every week, Zach drove to the library, where he dropped off a massive pile of books from the previous week and spent hours rebuilding a brand new and even more impressive pile that he'd read within a few hours. Then, he would drive to his second favorite location, Five Guys, where he would purchase the exact same order each week: one double patty hamburger with no cheese, lettuce, or tomato, but completely smothered in ketchup and pickles. It was weekly entertainment for me to watch him inhale it in less than a minute, lick his fingers clean, smile with satisfaction, and eagerly dive into his new stack of books. This routine has been consistent for the past six years.

Routine, consistency, and repetition are essential to Zach. Like many people with autism, Zach prefers when all activities and plans for the day, week, and month are scheduled. Spontaneity is not good for Zach. He doesn't like the unexpected.

He is much more comfortable with the predictability that comes with consistency and routine. With routines, he has time to make decisions because he repeatedly makes them every day. He doesn't need to think quickly or problem-solve a situation he isn't familiar with. This is one of the many reasons he enjoys his job as a cashier. At the grocery store, Zach knows exactly what he's supposed to do, and there are rarely any surprises.

But the challenges of autism are always present. Many autistic people struggle and must fight even harder to accomplish their goals. Some need a lot of extra help to do things that neurotypical people take for granted. Following complex directions, getting a good night of sleep, or even speaking out loud can prove difficult to those with severe ASD; yet there are also autistic people whose symptoms are minor enough to allow them to live their day-to-day lives with relative "normalcy." Everybody is different. Everybody is unique. It's a spectrum, after all.

And right now, you're probably thinking, "Hold it right there, Josh! Are you just going to skip over that part where you said autism gave Zach a superpower? Because that is quite a bold thing to say and then just forget to explain!" You're right. It is bold, but it's also true. Autism has given Zach a superpower.

Zach is one of the nicest people anyone could ever have the pleasure of meeting. His abundant and never-ending kindness is contagious, and he makes the world a better place. He's always willing to lend a hand to whomever needs it, no matter the circumstance, and he never asks for anything in return. He cares much more about the well-being of his family and co-workers than his own happiness. There are many (too many) times when I drag him home long after his shift has ended because he is concerned that the store will struggle without him. Oh, and I have to steer him clear of beggars for fear that he will offer them his entire wallet (which he has done). Our parents and I often remind him that it's perfectly acceptable to take a vacation day. It's healthy to take a break occasionally and focus on himself, but Zach struggles with this concept. I can't imagine a time when he isn't helping somebody or trying to make someone's day just that little bit better. This is Zach's superpower. It's simply who he is.

Zach does all of this without the ability to fly. He doesn't have super strength and can't run at the speed of light. He sometimes even has trouble opening the pickle jars that have been sitting in the back of the fridge for a little too long (but come on, who doesn't?). Zach has limits, like us all, but unlike so many of us (myself included), Zach is inspired by his limitations. He strives to make people's lives better: strangers, family, and friends alike. It doesn't matter to Zach. If there is a need, he will be the first in line to selflessly lend a hand. Isn't that what superheroes do?

Sadly, many people will never get to experience Zach's superpower. Some will take one glance at him and call him dumb or slow or mentally challenged. I've watched his customers sneer at him when he mispronounces a word and shout at him when he can't scan their items at the speed of light. I've seen his co-workers try to take advantage of him, manipulating him into lending them money because they know he is too nice to ask for it back or leaving the rest of their shifts to him because they know he will work until exhaustion. I've witnessed his managers ignoring the days he's requested off work and consistently scheduling him for the earliest mornings and latest nights because they know he will always show up.

When people don't understand something, they create their own truths about it, and that's what they decide to believe. I think, in many ways, it's easier for them to create a false narrative because it is uncomfortable to try to understand the unknown or unfamiliar. I've seen people look at Zach and create a narrative that he is dull or stupid or he's trying to hinder them in some way. Similar to how people write hurtful comments on social media because the anonymity of the Internet protects them from the ramifications. The people who judge Zach before they get to know him rationalize that they can treat him poorly because he won't fight back, call them out, or report their abuse. He just takes it because he doesn't ever want to hurt them or cause anyone pain in any way. He often doesn't even realize how he is being treated at all. If these people take two minutes to meet him, though, they'd see him for who he truly is.

This is my reason for writing this book. I want to educate people about ASD, highlight the effects it can have on people, and share ways to support family and community members who are on the autistic spectrum. More importantly, I want to showcase the unexpected brilliance that a person with autism might possess. After all, I already said that autism can give somebody a superpower, and Zach isn't the only person I know with an autistic superpower.

And most importantly, I'm writing this book to give every single reader a look behind the glasses and the goofy grin of my favorite person in the multiverse (which includes the Marvel and DC universes as well). Allow me to introduce Zach Stehle, my autistic brother, a superhero, and the greatest best friend anyone could ever have.

2

PARTNERS IN CRIME

Hey man, I have to tell you something. But whatever you do, don't tell Mom and Dad. Promise?
Zach

Of course, man. I promise.
Josh

Okay... now, seriously this time. Promise me you won't tell them.
Zach

[laughs] Yes Zach, I promise.
Josh

...I don't believe you.
Zach

I WILL NEVER FORGET THE FIRST TIME ZACH broke the law.

For twenty-two years straight, he did everything he could never to break a single rule. He never skipped a day of school or used more than his allotted fifteen minutes for lunch breaks at work. He never crossed the street without a crosswalk, never brushed his teeth with the water still running, and never, ever drove past a stop sign without making a complete stop and then looking both ways for other cars. (I can't say the same, can you?) Zach even waited until he was eighteen before he watched the movie *Deadpool* because it was rated R, and he wasn't old enough when it first came out. For twenty-two years straight, Zach maintained his perfect record. Then, on this one bitter night, his impeccable record went up in flames.

I wasn't there the night it happened. In fact, I didn't even know Zach had been pulled over by the police until weeks later, when he and I were driving to Five Guys for lunch.

He was acting differently that day. Usually, our car rides were filled with lively conversations about our favorite superheroes, movies, and video games. My conversations with Zach are always fun and generally laid back, but on that day, Zach was silent. He fidgeted uncomfortably with a piece of string that had become loose from his shirt and stared straight ahead as we drove. I sat quietly, waiting for Zach to gather his thoughts. Then, as I turned into the restaurant's parking lot, he cleared his throat.

"Josh," he said carefully. "I have to tell you something, but you can't tell Mom and Dad any of it."

I remember smiling reassuringly. "No problem, bud. It can be our secret."

He looked at me seriously. "You're sure?"

"I'm sure."

"Okay..." He nodded several times. "Well, two weeks ago, when I was driving home from the new Avengers movie, I..." He paused. "I got pulled over by ... a police officer." He whispered the last part, as if saying it any louder would land him in more trouble. I nearly spat out my gum. I was so proud.

"No way!" I said, unable to hold my grin. "What did he clock you for? Zach, that's amazing!"

"It's not amazing! I got in trouble!" Zach looked at me with confusion.

"Yeah, you did." I laughed, punching him lightly on the shoulder. "You're a criminal now, just like your brother!"

"J-o-o-s-h!" Zach pouted. He always elongated my name like that when he was annoyed at me. I laughed again.

"It's okay, man. Getting pulled over happens to everybody. It isn't really a big deal. If anything, this is good news."

He looked at me skeptically, knowing the punchline was about to come. "Why?"

"Because when we get pulled over tonight and they find all of my false identities, you'll know how to deal with it!"

"J-O-O-S-H!"

"Look, bud..." I said, preparing to give the greatest advice of my entire life. (Seriously, I'm proud of this one.) "Did you break the law? Yes. Technically, you did. But also no, you didn't because the speed limit is just a suggestion that doesn't really mean much. It's just a rule that most people don't like or, honestly, care about that much, except, of course, if they are in front of the police. The police enforce the speed limit, so you've got to go slow around them. But sometimes, even they don't care at all! So basically, what I'm trying to say is... it's okay."

(Yes, that's a direct quote. And yes, I am a fantastic influence.)

Zach shook his head. "But I didn't break the speed limit."

I remember glancing at him, an eyebrow raised.

"What?"

"I didn't break the speed limit. It was something else."

"Zach... then what in the world were you doing?"

[pause]

I'll get back to that story later, but this seems to be as good a time as any to explain some particulars of Zach:

1. As I mentioned in chapter one, Zach sometimes has a hard time understanding and appropriately handling "gray area" situations.

2. When it comes to breaking the law, Zach will never, ever intentionally do so.

Beginning with number one, when decisions are categorized as "gray area," it means that they cannot be solved through the simple application of ethics. There are no right or wrong factors to these situations, nothing completely good or bad that Zach can identify to determine the correct solution. What makes these situations so challenging is that they are nearly impossible to predict, which means that my family and I can't prepare him for every single situation he could possibly encounter.

Of course, Zach being unprepared with a repertoire of case scenarios can lead to his being placed in potentially dangerous circumstances. So, it has been important for Zach to practice decision-making skills, in general. Though uncomfortable and, more often than not, incredibly stressful, sometimes gray area situations can also lead to some unexpected (and absolutely hilarious) dilemmas as well.

Perhaps my favorite example of this is the story of Snapback Dude and the Nickel. Every week after Zach goes to the library to pick up his mountain of books, he drives to the nearby mall food court and purchases one Five Guys double patty burger with no cheese, lettuce, or tomato, but completely smothered in ketchup and pickles. That you already know.

What I haven't told you is that every so often, a beggar named Snapback Dude shows up in the food court parking lot and asks people for money. Of course, that isn't his actual name, but we all call him that because nobody has ever seen him without two snapback hats on his head. Most of the time, Snapback Dude just sits on a bench, far away from the entrance to Five Guys. Therefore, I had never thought to prepare Zach for a potential encounter with him.

Then one day, when Zach came home from his weekly library and Five Guys trip, he looked a little shaken. He walked into the kitchen, holding his greasy Five Guys bag in one hand and his wallet in the other hand, and sat down awkwardly at the table. At the time, my parents and I were sitting around the table, and we all noticed that he was acting particularly peculiar.

"What's going on, Zach?" my dad asked.

Zach glanced up at him. "Well, I went to Five Guys. And when I got out of my car, there was a beggar there, and he asked me for money."

"Snapback Dude..." I said under my breath and exchanged concerned looks with my parents. It was no secret that Zach is a ridiculously generous man. In fact, during our recent trip to Las Vegas, I had to walk him away from multiple beggars because he insisted on giving them "just a little bit" of cash, even though all he had were $20 bills. I remember shaking my head. If Zach had any extra money laying around, it was now, without a doubt, in the hands of Snapback Dude. Or, of course, the hands of Ghost, Snapback Dude's dealer. (That specific mall has a shady history.)

But I digress. We all looked at Zach and said in unison, "what happened?"

Zach shook his head. "Well, I didn't have any money to give him."

My mom breathed a sigh of relief. "That's okay, honey. You don't have to give beggars any money. So, you just ignored him?"

Zach shook his head again. "Well, not exactly... I gave him a nickel."

"You gave the beggar a nickel?" my mom exclaimed.

"Yep. It was the most I could find."

You read that correctly. Zach gave Snapback Dude a *nickel*. Imagine being a beggar, with nothing but the clothes on your back and the snapback hats on your head, and some cocky kid gives you a nickel to help get you back on your feet. With only nineteen more, you can afford half of a hot dog! With one thousand, four hundred and twenty-six more, you can afford a night in the local Holiday Inn! I thought it was hilarious.

Then Zach, confused, looked at us. He genuinely thought he had helped somebody in need. The problem was that he felt bad he couldn't give the beggar more than five cents.

The story gets a little scary when you consider how a different beggar might have reacted to a situation like that. Luckily, Snapback Dude didn't seem to care. If he had taken offense, and even retaliated, how could Zach have defended himself? Zach thought he was doing the right thing. Unfortunately, neither I nor my parents had the foresight to predict and prepare him for a situation like that. After all, how could we have?

Zach has improved at gray area decision making with time and practice. As he has grown older, he has begun to understand better how to identify some of the complexities of various situations and how to make informed choices accordingly. However, there is one, very, very, extremely large exception to this.

Now, regarding number two on the list above, Zach is absolutely terrible at dealing with decisions in which he might be required to break the law.

Please understand, I am not advocating for criminal activity. In fact, I've never been *caught* doing anything illegal in my life. But even a saint such as I can understand that occasionally, a law, or let's say a rule, or heck, even a legal suggestion, may need to be broken to correctly handle a situation. Zach doesn't quite comprehend this. His black and white thinking precludes his ability to justify breaking a law, no matter the cost.

I remember one time in particular when this personality trait almost got us into serious, life-threatening trouble. Zach was driving down the road one night, and I was in the passenger seat. It was an early Friday evening, right around that time when everybody was in a mad rush to get home and start the weekend.

Everybody except for Zach. Zach wasn't worried about getting home any quicker than the law allowed. He obeyed the speed limit and was driving that exact speed down the single-lane road.

As you can probably imagine, it didn't take long for a line of cars to pile up behind us, all impatiently driving at Zach's speed. Despite my encouragement to hit the gas, Zach refused to drive any faster than what was posted on the speed limit signs. So that line of cars continued to grow until we had nothing short of a parade following behind us.

Then we got to a stop light, the first we'd seen in miles. Initially, the light was green, and Zach maintained his speed. As we approached, that light turned yellow.

Yellow lights are difficult for Zach because they require split-second decision-making skills, and making the wrong call could result in disaster, injury, or a minor criminal offense. So, as we approached the yellow light, Zach decided we were going to be able to make it into the intersection before the light turned red and maintained his speed. The car behind us, anxious to get home, had a similar idea and hugged us as we smoothly drove through the intersection.

Just kidding. We didn't drive through the intersection at all. At the last possible moment, the traffic light turned red. Zach slammed on the brakes, causing us both to launch forward in our seats and causing the car behind us to swerve violently to the right to avoid slamming into us at 40 miles per hour.

Once my initial panic passed, I remember looking at Zach in shock. Amazingly, he seemed quite calm. He had avoided running the red light and, therefore, avoided breaking the law. In his mind, he had done the right thing. Needless to say, the driver blaring his horn in the grass did not agree.

This is the extent to which Zach refuses to break the law. He believes that he should never, ever do it. Even when I explained to him later why that experience was dangerous, it was tough for him to justify any other course of action other than the one he had chosen. In Zach's mind, he had followed the rules.

I often reflect on this story with mixed emotions. Like anybody, I would rather have a sibling who is transfixed on following rules, rather than yet another one who is transfixed on breaking them. (Yup, I'm calling out my twin sister. Sorry, Becca!) But as Zach's brother, it's my responsibility to help prepare Zach for the real world, and the real world doesn't always follow the rules. The real world is one large gray area situation.

Fortunately, Zach's obsession with obeying the law does mean that he will never intentionally get into any legal trouble. However, remember that particularly bitter night I mentioned earlier?

[rewind]

Zach shook his head. "But I didn't break the speed limit."

I remember glancing at him, an eyebrow raised. "What?"

"I didn't break the speed limit. It was something else."

"Zach... then what in the world were you doing?"

[resume]

Zach shrugged his shoulders aggressively. He always did that when he had trouble explaining something. "I was driving the speed limit, and the cop pulled me over. He said I was going too slow and was holding up traffic. I don't know." Zach shook his head. "I didn't know I was breaking a rule."

I stroked my chin thoughtfully, pretending I had a beard. "Hmm. Zach, which lane were you driving in?"

Zach looked up at me. "The lane... closest to the middle?" He put up his thumb and pointer finger in each hand and picked out the one that made an "L." "The left lane."

I grinned. "Ah, I see now. On a highway, the left lane is the fast lane. This means that when you're driving on that side, it is actually expected that you drive faster than the posted speed limit. That's why the cop pulled you over."

"Yeah, I think he did explain that to me," Zach said sadly. "But that's a dumb rule."

"Many rules are," I remember saying. "Did the cop give you a ticket?"

"No, he just gave me a warning and told me to drive home safely. I don't think I'm in trouble."

I smiled at him. "You're not, bud. Don't worry."

"But that still doesn't mean that you get to tell Mom and Dad!"

I grinned mischievously. "I'll think about it."

"J-o-o-s-h!"

"Okay. I promise I won't tell them."

3

WHAT IS AUTISM?

> You know you're autistic, right?
> **Josh**

> Of course I know I'm autistic. You know
> I'm autistic, right?
> **Zach**

> [laughs] Yes, I know.
> **Josh**

21

FROM OCTOBER 2021 TO MARCH 2022, DURING the second year of the global COVID-19 pandemic when I was finally able to be around people again, I conducted research at my former university, Arcadia University, in Pennsylvania. I bought a big, college-ruled notebook (because it made me feel smarter than a wide-ruled notebook) and a box of fancy gel pens. On the top of the first page, I wrote in big block letters:

WHAT IS AUTISM?

During those six months, I interviewed over one hundred people and asked each of them this one, single question, "What is Autism?" I told them not to give me an answer they thought I was looking for, but, instead, to use this question to start a conversation. There were no right or wrong answers, as long as the answers were genuine.

My interviewees came from many different walks of life. Some just happened to be my closest friends. Others were complete strangers. For some interviews, I set a date and time and explained beforehand why we were meeting, and I recorded their every word. But other times, I asked the question spontaneously, without explaining anything to the unknowing interviewee. These random encounters often led to the best and most eye-opening conversations. After each interview, I recorded their responses into my fat, college-ruled notebook. Over one hundred responses, each of them different, each of them unique.

Why?

Since the moment I was born, understanding autism has been an instrumental part of my life. Due to my incredibly close connection with my brother, as well as other friends who are also on the spectrum, I've been closely connected to the disorder and the autism awareness community.

However, it wasn't until I went away to college that I truly began to discover the disconnect and misguided prejudice that many people have regarding Autistic Spectrum Disorder. Of course, this isn't true of all people, and, oftentimes, it's not intentional. Nonetheless, it *is* there.

I remember my third day at Arcadia University so clearly. It was around lunchtime, and I had planned to meet up with a new friend, Dan, at the university dining hall. The hall was bustling that day, so we ended up sitting with some of our mutual acquaintances. Since we were all getting to know each other, the conversation was superficial. We talked about sports, particularly basketball, and how our school's team was supposed to be really amazing that year. (I was a member of that basketball team, and, no, we weren't amazing at all.) Then, our conversation moved to the NBA, and, specifically, my favorite basketball player, Danny Green.

Now, Danny Green is by no means the greatest basketball player in the world. In fact, whenever I mention to NBA fans that he is my favorite player, I am always met with the same bug-eyed reaction and drawn out "Him??" followed by "He's garbage!" or "He sucks!" But on this day, Dan hit me with a slightly different response:

"Him? He runs like a kid with autism!"

It was said so naturally, so passively, that I nearly missed it at first. Dan's comment got a chuckle from the group, and then the conversation moved on, as if he had never said it at all.

However, that single sentence stuck with me for the rest of the day. Of course, it wasn't the first time I had heard autism being used as the butt of a joke. I went to high school, after all. This was just the first time I realized how commonplace it was for unintentional prejudice toward autism to happen. There was no ill intent behind the comment, and Dan wasn't trying to be mean. He said those words purely because it was something that "people just said."

I have had many experiences in life in which I have witnessed prejudice toward those with ASD. I have witnessed in classrooms and on university street corners people openly mocking individuals on the autistic spectrum. I have sat in rooms in which people threw around the word "retard" as if were a compliment, and I have stood in line at Zach's grocery store and stared in disbelief as the person in front of me called my brother stupid and incompetent to his face.

Yet, to me, this conversation with Dan was more concerning than anything I had ever experienced before.

In life, there will always be people who needlessly attack others, using vile and unnecessary language with the sole intent to cause pain. However, when hurtful language becomes so commonplace that average, kind, and neurotypical individuals such as Dan use autism as an insult without realizing the impact of their word choice, then disrespect becomes normalized. It becomes something that "people just say."

From that day forward, I learned to listen more closely to the words people use. I sat in the back of classrooms and hallways, and I became hypervigilant when people used autism as the butt of a joke or the ending of a hateful remark. Again, I knew and understood that these comments were rarely said with malice toward people on the spectrum. Regardless, these words were being tossed around in everyday language, and they were hurtful.

At the end of each day, I made lists of the things that I'd heard. I began asking people to elaborate on what they had said and why they chose those particular words to communicate their thoughts. Then, the margins of my marketing notebook became too small... or, maybe, my new project became too big. So, I drove to Target and bought that big, new notebook and box of fancy gel pens. On the top of the very first page, I wrote in big block letters:

WHAT IS AUTISM?

I wanted to ask anybody and everybody. I wanted, no, *needed* to understand how a mental disorder affecting over 75,000,000 people had become a run-of-the-mill insult among college kids. I *needed* to know why autism awareness and acceptance were treated like jokes among individuals who were typically kind to people in need. I needed to understand how a friend like Dan, who volunteered at a food bank during the weekends and even let me borrow his car once when mine was in the shop (I almost drove it into a ditch) could be so unaware of the hurtful impact of his word choices.

Was it a lack of knowledge regarding ASD? Was it a lack of acceptance? Was it a lack of experience with autistic individuals that caused people to assume certain things about autism that weren't true? For those who disrespected autism, both intentionally and unintentionally, perhaps it was a combination of all three.

Luckily, I was in college, and college is an opportunistic place for a college guy like me to find and talk to just about anybody. So, I wandered around my school with my notebook and my fancy gel pens, and I did just that. I talked to people, or, rather, I listened to people. The day after I bought my new supplies, I conducted my very first interview. I was walking back to my dorm room after eating too many cookies in the dining hall when I spotted my friend, "Tony Stark." Immediately, I grabbed my notebook and approached him.

Interview 1: Tony Stark

Subject: Tony was a member of a sports team at Arcadia University. To protect his identity, Tony's name has been changed to that of Iron Man's alter ego.

Josh: Tony!

Tony: Josh!

Josh: Tony, I'm doing a survey. Can you answer a question for me?

Tony: Dang, I hate questions. But okay.

Josh: What is autism?

Tony: **What do you mean? Like the disease?**

Josh: ...

Tony: It's a disease, right?

Tony wasn't the only interviewee to mistakenly call autism a disease. Of the approximately one hundred college students interviewed in this experiment, 95% correctly identified autism as a neurological disorder. However, other recorded responses included "disease," "mental block," and "unknown."

I was happy to see that most of the interviewees had a baseline understanding of ASD, but some lacked even the most basic knowledge. When asked to provide symptoms of autism, 90% of students were able to identify three or more, while 10% provided two or fewer. Of the many autistic symptoms, the three that were most often mentioned by the students were obsessive interests, repetitive behaviors, and savant syndrome.

I continued by asking interviewees to elaborate on what they knew about autism (always using the same line, "tell me more..."), and the interviewees then began to branch off into different areas. It was common for the interviewees to discuss the symptoms of autism in more detail, often focusing on the personal experiences they've had with autistic friends or family members or describing the unique skills of the famous savants they had witnessed online. Others focused on special education and the unique skillsets often required to be successful in that field as an educator or paraprofessional.

"Special education teachers aren't often in charge of large classrooms and tons of students," I remember a girl saying. "Instead, these teachers are instructing students who may not learn in the same way as their public-school friends."

Many interviewees didn't know much more about autism outside of the most basic facts, though. Sometimes, watching these students rack their brains for a few moments before giving up was disheartening. Often, they flashed me a short smile or shrugged indifferently.

"Maybe I need to do a little more research," one friend of mine commented after our interview. "My cousin is autistic, but I don't know him very well."

Nineteen interviewees were unaware that autism has no cure. Tony Stark was particularly shocked by this fact. When I mentioned it to him, he stared at me with wide eyes and said, "Oh, dang! Aight."

But the point of my interviews was not to ask simple questions and record simple responses. I wanted to create dialogues. After starting the initial conversations, I opened the floor to the interviewees and asked them to elaborate.

"How do you treat an autistic person in public?" I asked a girl once as we were sitting on the benches in the quad between classes.

"Well, just like anybody else," she replied.

"Why?"

"Because they *are* anybody else. When I go out, I guess I just try to be considerate to everybody. If there's somebody in a wheelchair,

I'll hold open the door for them. If there's somebody in a rush to get somewhere, I'll get out of their way. And if there's somebody who is on the spectrum and needs help or patience or anything, I'll do my best to provide it. I feel like if we follow specific rules about how to help or approach autistic people, it's insincere. It'll make them feel different or lesser, like they always need help or have to follow special rules. Why can't everyone just, instead, be considerate to everyone else's needs?"

I enjoyed that dialogue.

As my research progressed, I encountered many interviewees who had very interesting thoughts, ideas, and messages to convey.

Interview 11: Peter Parker

Subject: Peter was a member of an esports team at Arcadia University. To protect his identity, Peter's name has been changed to that of Spiderman's alter ego.

Josh: Do you have personal experience with autism or autism awareness?

Peter: It's what I'm studying. I want to be in special education.

Josh: What inspired you to pursue that?

Peter: Nobody else gives these people a chance, so *I'm* going to.

I knew right away that Peter was going to make a difference in the autism community. When he spoke about his focus in special education, he was knowledgeable, yet humble. He also seemed incredibly determined, as if nothing was going to stop him from achieving his goal.

———

Peter: I've never liked standardized tests or lectures. What's the point of hammering one style of teaching into a million styles of learning?

Josh: Yeah, I like that. It makes you think... If only I was actually good at teaching.

Peter: [shakes his head] You don't have to be a teacher to be in special ed! Be a counselor, or a school psychologist, or an educational writer. We always need people!

Josh: You're right.

———

Other interviewees provided answers that were so powerful they changed my outlook on autism on a grand scale and even shaped entire chapters of this book.

Interview 72: Diana Prince

Subject: Diana was a friend of mine at Arcadia University. To protect her identity, Diana's name has been changed to that of Wonder Woman's alter ego.

Josh: Why is autism awareness important?

Diana: Because autistic people deserve it. They are so unique, special, and amazing; but there are people out there who will do everything they can to abuse them or take advantage of them. It is our job as a community to protect against those people, and we do that by being a voice so powerful that they are forced to rethink their beliefs and actions toward the autism community.

Josh: How do we build a voice like that?

Diana: Well, you're writing a book. That's a good start.

———

She's right. Writing a book is a good start, but it isn't enough. Not even close.

One of the most revealing aspects of the interview process was the disconnect between those who were connected to autism in some way and those who weren't. The interviewees who had personal experience with autism were exceedingly more educated on the subject matter, were more inclined to ask questions, and were more likely to engage in deeper conversation. On the other hand, many of the interviewees who had little to no experience didn't understand much and were content to keep it that way. For some, the subject of autism even made them seem uncomfortable or annoyed.

Creating a lasting change requires everybody who belongs to the human race to do as Diana said, "rethink their beliefs and actions toward the autistic community." It requires being loud, outspoken, and, most importantly, consistent. Conducting these interviews proved to me that reading one book or hearing one word from a member of our community is not enough to create the kind of change needed to make a ripple in people's understanding of autism. Spreading awareness and acceptance of autism must be a lifelong endeavor. This includes advocating for those with mental disabilities, volunteering and attending special needs events, spreading autism awareness messages on social media platforms, and educating others about the movement. And, yes, of course, writing a book about being a superhero expert.

We can build this voice, but we must do it together.

As Diana and I were wrapping up our conversation in the dining hall, a worker holding a broom and dustpan walked over to us.

"We're closing up now. Y'all got to get out," she said.

I glanced down at my phone. "Oh, my goodness," I said. "We've been doing this interview for three hours!"

Thank you, Diana.

Then, of course, there was my favorite interview of all.

Interview 94: Steve Rogers

Subject: Steve was a friend of mine at Arcadia University. To protect his identity, Steve's name has been changed to that of Captain America's alter ego.

Josh: What is autism?

Steve: Autism is a gift.

Josh: Why?

Steve: Are you kidding? Have you seen those YouTube videos of that guy playing like two pianos at once? The dude is nuts!

I remember jotting down a note reminding myself to dedicate a chapter of this book to Steve Rogers, because he's exactly right. Autism *is* a gift. If you're intrigued by this, flip to chapter 6 (or continue reading and you'll get there soon enough).

By the time I left Arcadia University for the summer, I was prepared to write this book, and, more importantly, I was *excited* to write this book. I had learned more from talking to people and hearing their unique points of view about autism than I could have ever learned from most websites or research articles. I had experienced the expansive range of knowledge that my community possessed about ASD, and I knew what the message, purpose, and goal of my book needed to be.

4

EXPERTISE

Close your eyes. I'm about to do something highly illegal.
Josh

No, no, no-no-no-no!
Zach

[illegally turns onto a highway]
Josh

33

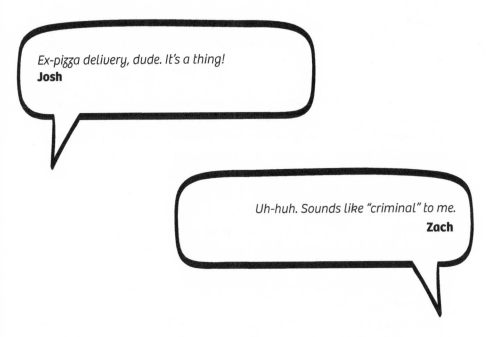

> Ex-pizza delivery, dude. It's a thing!
> **Josh**

> Uh-huh. Sounds like "criminal" to me.
> **Zach**

"I AM A SUPERHERO EXPERT. YOU ARE NOT."

The first time Zach said those words to me, it was like being armless and legless, locked in a cage, next to a hungry lion who loves the taste of human flesh. As much as I struggled and screamed and tried to get away, with no arms or legs, I was helpless to the wrath of the ravenous beast.

Yeah... I should probably elaborate on that one. I'm not being melodramatic in the least.

When Zach said those words to me a few years ago, we were sitting on the floor in his room, watching YouTube videos and debating superheroes.

"Josh, I am a superhero expert. You are not."

He said it matter-of-factly and so completely devoid of emotion, except for that hint of smugness that only an expert in his field could have. When it came to superheroes, my brother had me outmatched, and we both knew it.

But that didn't stop me from trying to best him. We were watching "Death Battle," a popular YouTube show which pitted two fictional comic book characters against each other in fights to the death. Zach enjoyed watching the show because each

35

episode provided extensive analysis of both characters' abilities, fighting styles, techniques, weaponry, and experience, giving the viewer all of the information needed in order to be able to choose a victor of the battle. The show's two hosts, nicknamed "Wizard" and "Boomstick," took the comics, films, and all other media portraying these characters very seriously, which Zach appreciated. I, on the other hand, enjoyed watching the show because I had a 50/50 shot of choosing the winner each time. "Death Battle" concluded each episode with an extravagantly bloody and over-the-top battle to the death, in which only one of the two characters survived. In the end, Wizard and Boomstick explained in detail why the victorious character had won and what challenges each character had faced. Then, they wrapped everything up with some cheesy banter before directing the viewers to another episode. In other words, this show was utter YouTube perfection.

For those who haven't heard of "Death Battle," these videos are more addictive than movie theater popcorn, puppy GIFs, and even chocolate fountains. Needless to say, Zach and I were hooked.

However, I do have a problem with these videos. More specifically, I have a problem with watching them with Zach.

See, Zach is not a member of "Death Battle's" target audience. That is, people like me, who enjoy comic book characters and gory action sequences but who also have absolutely no way to reliably or accurately predict who is going to win each battle. The problem with Zach is that, before all the extensive analysis is shown and before many of the episodes are even published, Zach already knows who is going to win. Every. Single. Time. While most viewers are expected to view the analysis to help them pick who they believe is going to be victorious, Zach is hardly ever exposed to a piece of information he hasn't already considered. Sometimes, he even points out information that Wizard and Boomstick have missed about the characters if he believes they have neglected to mention a minor detail. Zach is a true superhero expert, and by the time the characters engage in battle, the outcome is just a formality to him.

But this doesn't stop him from watching the show more often than a teenager scrolls on Instagram. This dynamic has always confused me. So, one day, while Zach was slouched, reading a comic book in his favorite bean bag chair, I asked him why he even watched "Death Battle" at all if he already knew exactly what was going to happen.

"Simple," Zach replied. "I know what should happen. I just watch to make sure they don't mess it up!"

"That's confident," I remember saying to him. He just shrugged, before burying his head back into his comic.

I pursed my lips together. I knew better than to question Zach in his area of expertise, but another part of me simply had to put my brother to the test. I grabbed my phone from my pocket and pulled up the YouTube app, scrolling through the long list of "Death Battle" episodes on the channel until I found what I was looking for. It was a "Death Battle" video that neither of us had seen before: Hawkeye vs. Green Arrow.

"Zach-Attack! Tell me, who is going to win this one?" I asked, pulling him away from his comic book and shoving my phone in his face.

"Hey, I'm reading!" he said, reaching for his book, which I kicked out of the way.

"No. This is much more important. Who is going to win? Hawkeye or Green Arrow?"

Zach paused, scratching his head in thought. "Well... Hawk... hmm, this is interesting."

"Aha!" I exclaimed. "A 'Death Battle' you cannot solve!"

"Not so fast." Zach replied. "Green Arrow has a lot more trick arrows, but Hawkeye has a much more powerful bow. Two times as powerful, in fact. Both are excellent shots, but Hawkeye does tend to get hit more often than Green Arrow does, and he can fire at machine gun speeds, at least in the comics. Hawkeye at his best is probably better... I'd go with Hawkeye."

I pursed my lips. "Okay. I'll go with Green Arrow, then. I've always thought Hawkeye was a little lame, anyway."

Zach shrugged. "Alright."

He pressed play, and the "Death Battle" began. Wizard and Boomstick started with Green Arrow and wasted no time rattling off his abilities and backstory. As they dove deeper into the superhero analysis, I began to get excited. After all, it was revealed that Green Arrow carried around *atomic warhead explosive arrows* in his quiver, along with many other weapons of mass destruction.

Yep. The guy that Zach did not pick had apparently strapped nuclear warheads to the ends of arrows. Talk about coming prepared for a battle! I definitely didn't remember seeing Hawkeye do that in the Avengers movies. I was confident I would win this "Death Battle." Finally, Zach the superhero expert would be defeated!

"Why don't we just skip to the battle, dude," I said, grabbing the phone and sliding to the second half of the video. "I know I'm going to win, anyway."

"Well, you can be disappointed now or later," Zach replied seriously. "Hawkeye has better weaponry than Green Arrow. He's also faster and stronger. Green Arrow may have the edge in hand-to-hand combat due to his training under Natas, but Hawkeye trained with Natasha Romanoff. You know, Black Widow? He can catch an arrow with his bare hands. He even did it when he went blind, which happened in two different storylines."

"Alright, alright, I've heard enough," I replied, and we returned to the video.

Sure enough, as soon as I pressed play, Zach's words began to slowly come true on the small screen in front of us. After a short skirmish, a Hawkeye-propelled arrow cleaved its way through Green Arrow's body, splitting my chosen superhero in two.

"Told you," Zach said, the hint of a smirk on his face.

"I don't get it!" I exclaimed. "Green Arrow has nuclear warhead arrows! And punching glove arrows! All kinds of arrows! He should have won!"

Zach shrugged. "I am a superhero expert. You are not."

And with that, he returned to his comic book.

Well, I guess that is what happens when you challenge an expert. I shook my head and resumed the video. Wizard and Boomstick's post-battle analysis always did a great job reminding me just how much I had yet to learn about superheroes.

And that is when Zach's genius truly struck me.

———

[16:24] [2]

[Announcer] Hawkeye wins!

[Wizard] Shot for shot, arrow for arrow, Green Arrow and Hawkeye are a well-made match, making this an extremely close fight.

[Boomstick] Green Arrow has pulled off some ridiculous shots, but when Hawkeye is at his best, it's nearly impossible for any mortal man to hit him. We're talking about a guy who <u>catches arrows in his bare hands, even when he's been blinded.</u>

[Wizard] Both archers wield impressive bows, too. An average bow needs as much as 80 pounds of force to pull. Green Arrow's bow has an impressive draw weight of 125 pounds. <u>However, Hawkeye's is double that, at 250 pounds.</u> This is the same bow he can fire at near <u>machine gun speeds,</u> even at a faster rate than Green Arrow, while wearing chainmail.

[Boomstick] Green Arrow <u>may have an arrow for just about any situation,</u> but he didn't have one for making him <u>faster, stronger, and tougher</u> than Hawkeye. Looks like Green Arrow got shafted!

[Wizard] The winner is Hawkeye!

———

I scrolled back the video and watched this post-fight analysis for a second time and then a third. It was like déjà vu. Everything

---

[2] YouTube, "Death Battle," https://www.youtube.com/watch?v=KehZYhoa6lk

Zach had just said was being repeated in the video. Every point that Wizard and Boomstick made, every reason that Hawkeye had for winning that battle, Zach had already mentioned before even watching the battle.

I glanced back over at him, shaking my head in wonder because Zach should not be capable of such a feat. Zach does not have a great memory. When he is required to perform quick cognitive actions, such as remembering all the letters in the alphabet or basic mathematics, he struggles.

Completing multiple-step instructions can also be difficult for my brother. Zach has a limitless supply of superhero knowledge, but he struggles to remember how to cook a piece of chicken or pasta, even though I have shown him how to do it multiple times. Zach can easily quote hundreds of episodes of superhero shows by memory, but he is unable to drive to a random location without a GPS, even if he has been to that location multiple times. Zach remembers everything about superheroes, but the real world is very different from the worlds of his comic books.

Zach struggles with this concept.

I must add, although superheroes are Zach's greatest passion, his selectively photographic memory isn't related purely to comic books. In fact, Zach has fallen in love with all kinds of fictional media and spends hours a day reading various book genres. Along with Marvel and DC comics, Zach is also a massive self-proclaimed *Star Wars* geek, a proud *Harry Potter* muggle, and an avid *The Lord of the Rings* nerd. His bookshelves are piled high with countless fantasy and science fiction books, and he has read them all at least a dozen times. On many occasions, I have grabbed the most random and arbitrary book from one of the seven bookcases around his room and begun reading a random line from the middle. Before I've even finished the sentence, Zach has always been able to tell me which book I have been reading, what was happening at that point of the book, who was speaking, which characters were in the scene, and even *which chapter I was on*. Yet, if I instead were to ask him to tell me the names of a few of my friends, he'd most likely be unable to do so, even if he had met them on several previous occasions. The point is that it is all about context when referring to Zach's ability to remember.

There was a time not too long ago when I really needed Zach to recall several names. I was hosting a pool party and had invited all my closest friends. Of course, Zach was my first invite, and I really wanted him to hang out with the other people and me at the party and have a good time. Luckily, included on that list of my friends was a name I knew he'd remember: "Sean McGuire."

Sean McGuire was one of my roommates at Arcadia University, back when I was still trying to make it as a basketball player. He is a very smart guy, an above-average golfer on the below-average Arcadia golf team, and an absolute class act. We quickly became good friends, and when he met Zach, Sean was an instant favorite. Before long, Sean was talking to Zach on the phone weekly about superheroes and comic books, brainstorming his own heroes and villains, and even taking Zach out for burgers and fries on several occasions. My brother loved Sean, but still, sometimes, he had trouble remembering his name.

Then, Sean and Zach got together for a night on the town. In other words, it was a trip to the local burger spot for a double patty burger with no cheese, lettuce, or tomato, but completely smothered in ketchup and pickles. While they were hanging out, they devised a list of superpowers Sean would have if he were a superhero. After a long discussion, they landed on Sean having the ability to fly... *and* phase through objects, *and* shoot spiky pro-jectiles, *and* possess enhanced strength, *and* display enhanced speed. (Of course, they did this because they were both greedy and needed to have every superpower to ever exist.) After talking for a long time and consuming many burgers, they finally figured out a name for their new magnum opus superhero: Ghosthawk.

Since that day, Zach has never forgotten Sean McGuire's name.

An "autism expert" meeting Zach for the first time would probably conclude that Zach learned Sean's name due to con-tinual exposure. That "expert" would be wrong. Zach learned Sean's name based on the context in which it was presented. He will never, ever forget Ghosthawk's true identity.

Perhaps that dynamic symbolizes the unfortunate truth about diagnosing autism. Given the vastness of the symptoms of ASD, and how wide the range of the autistic spectrum can be, there is no true diagnostic measure that best defines autism.

For example, listed below are WebMD's symptoms of autism. Please note that WebMD[3] clearly states that "if your child is on the spectrum, they **might** show some social symptoms by the time they're 8 to 10 months old." Symptoms include:

- Inability to respond to their name by their first birthday

- Disinterest in playing, sharing, or talking with other people

- Preference to be alone

- Avoidance or rejection of physical contact, including hugging

- Avoidance of eye contact

- Preference not to be comforted when they're upset

- Confusion regarding emotions – their own or others'

- Absence of desire to be picked up or guided with walking

- Delayed speech and language skills

- Flat, robotic speaking voice or singsong voice

- Echolalia (repeating the same phrase over and over)

- Problems with pronouns (saying "you" instead of "I," for example)

- Difficulty using common gestures (pointing or waving) and not responding to them

- Inability to stay on topic when talking or answering questions

- Difficulty recognizing sarcasm or joking

---

[3] WebMD: "Causes and Symptoms of Autism," https://www.webmd.com/brain/autism/symptoms-of-autism

- Trouble expressing needs and emotions
- Difficulty getting signals from body language, tone of voice, and expressions
- Constant moving (pacing) and "hyper" behavior
- Fixations on certain activities or objects
- Specific routines or rituals (and getting upset when a routine is changed, even slightly)
- Extreme sensitivity to touch, light, and sound
- Absence of "make-believe" play or imitating others' behaviors
- Fussy eating habits
- Lack of coordination, clumsiness

WebMD has made it abundantly clear that any of these symptoms *might* be signs of autism, or they *might* not be. Of course, there is always the possibility that a potentially autistic child could have many of these symptoms and not have ASD in any form. There is also just as likely a chance that a seemingly non-autistic child who is indeed on the autism spectrum could experience multiple symptoms that do not present on this list at all.

At the end of the day, there is no definitive list of autistic symptoms anywhere in the world that can accurately represent Zach's autism, or anybody's autism, as far as I can tell. Zach's autism affects him in his own way, and it varies wildly from the millions of other autistic people everywhere. Of course, some patterns exist throughout the autistic community. There are multiple symptoms that many people with ASD exhibit but there is no one true answer to the question, "What is Autism?" Everybody is unique. Everybody is different. That includes everybody on the spectrum as well.

Often when I tell people my brother is autistic, they respond with sympathy and even apologize like this is something bad or something they wouldn't wish on anyone. I have never understood this. It is true that people with ASD can't just get a prescription pill and make themselves neurotypical. **There is no cure.** They also can't always follow the same steps that a different person with autism could have followed to be successful. What Zach needs to be successful are clear rules to follow, a strong family support system, and plenty of time to himself; and this may be completely different from somebody else with autism. In this sense, autism can be really, really difficult, not only for people on the spectrum but also for the parents, siblings, family, friends, co-workers, and everybody else who simply want to provide their loved ones with the best possible lives.

But autism can also be really, really beautiful. There are immense joys that autism can bring to life from things as minuscule as comic books, or following rules, or helping people. Autism can transform the ways that people see the world. Zach does not judge those around him. He simply tries every day to make a positive impact on his community. Autism can alter how people approach challenges, allowing them to tackle obstacles in new, different, and unique ways. Zach uses the gifts that autism provides him to his advantage, relating key concepts and people in his life to superheroes in order to recall their names at the next encounter.

Autism can also give people incredible gifts and astonishing cognitive abilities. Many of the greatest and most indescribable feats of humankind come from members of the autism community and display what the human spirit is truly and fully capable of. (I know I already said it in the last chapter, but once again, if you are intrigued about this, flip to chapter 6. Or, of course, continue reading. I promise, it's coming up.)

ASD may present many challenges for my brother, but it also gives him a purpose, a love, and a wealth of interests. It has led him to find a community that he cares about passionately and that he has contributed to immensely.

Autism has also allowed Zach to excel at something in a way that few others could ever dream of achieving. His superhero knowledge is positively unmatched. His "Death Battle" success rate is as close to 100% as anyone could get. I mean, who in the right mind would be stupid enough to challenge him to a superhero prediction?

Oh, wait. That's me.

"I'm smarter than you when it comes to Marvel and DC stuff," Zach said to me once, after beating me in another "Death Battle" prediction. "But you're smarter at a whole lot of stuff... like basketball! You're the best basketball player ever! Even better than Michael Jordan!"

"I know man. I know," I replied. "But you're sure I'm not smarter than you at superheroes?"

"Umm, no," Zach said. "When it comes to superheroes, you're like a guy with no arms or legs locked in a cage, and I'm a hungry lion that loves the taste of human flesh. No matter how hard you try, I shred you to bits!"

His words, not mine.

5

MY BROTHER HAS AUTISM

What time does your manager's shift start tomorrow?
Josh

Josh, please, let me handle this.
Zach

I'm not just going to keep letting them do this to you. It's not going to happen.
Josh

> *I know, but you have to let me handle it.*
> *My way.*
> **Zach**

> ...
> **Josh**

> *Please.*
> **Zach**

> *Fine. But I'm going to be here with my phone, and if thereare any problems, you call me. Immediately. Not Mom. Not Dad. Me. Got it?*
> **Josh**

> *There won't be any problems. But alright.*
> **Zach**

MY BROTHER HAS AUTISM.

So, to Zach's past employees, I'm sorry if you thought I was overprotective or annoying when I questioned you about something Zach was being told to do.

To the friends who told me I was distant, I'm sorry if I wasn't always there when you asked for me. Zach needed my help, and it had nothing to do with you.

And to the people who said I wasn't giving them enough time, I'm sorry that you weren't my first priority.

But my brother has autism, and it is my responsibility to protect him.

To Zach's old manager, I'm sorry if you thought I had overstepped my boundaries by confronting you, even though we both knew you took advantage of him every chance you got. Maybe I did, but I didn't care. At the end of the day, we both understood that he would have rather dropped dead than disappoint you, so you abused his time and effort. But you didn't see his anxiety-ridden, sleepless nights in which he refused to talk to anyone yet had to get out of bed at five the next morning just to do it all over again. You didn't hear him when he said he hated his job and then blamed himself. You didn't know the impact you had on his life. You didn't understand.

To the man who stood behind Zach and me at the burger shop that day, I'm sorry that you had to wait in line a little longer while my brother was ordering his food. I get it. You were hungry, and you hadn't eaten since lunch; but no amount of your dirty looks and disgruntled sighs would have made me cut him off mid-sentence and order his meal for him. You waited your turn like everybody else, and you survived. It was just a cheeseburger and a couple of seconds of your time.

And to the people in my life who I no longer speak to, I'm sorry that I won't be your friend anymore. But you say the word "retard." The first few times, I let it go. I explained what the word meant, and I asked that you not use it anymore. I could only give you so many chances before I had to stop reminding you to use a different word and start reminding myself to find different friends. You all made it clear. You disrespected my brother, and you disrespected me.

I'm sorry if all of you feel differently, but my brother has autism. It is my responsibility to protect him.

This message isn't meant for everybody, but it is meant for more than just the people that I've specified. It is meant for people who have disrespected the autistic community. It is meant for people who think it is funny to mock a person with a mental disability (or *any* disability). **And it is meant for people who have witnessed these acts and stood by silently, allowing them to happen.**

Nobody is perfect, and everybody faces their own unique challenges. Personally, I can talk for hours about anything to anybody, and I can reliably throw a basketball into a hoop from an obnoxious distance away. However, my memory is worse than a goldfish's, and I'm a notoriously slow reader. Zach, on the other hand, has a brilliant Superhero encyclopedia memory and is the fastest reader I know. However, he struggles to maintain eye contact during conversation, and he doesn't have the motor skills to even come close to making a layup.

One of us has challenges related to autism. One of us does not. Therefore, we both have challenges.

So, to the man at the burger shop that day, things could have been different. If you had only realized that your ability to speak clearly did not automatically make you better at life than somebody who struggles to pronounce their words. If you had only tried to understand a little more about the person you glared at. If only you had only known what kind of a man that person was. If you had cared just a little, perhaps you would have acted differently.

But you didn't care.

All you knew was that he was different. And you were right.

My brother has autism.

6

AUTISM IS A GIFT

Thousands of years ago, one of the many Divines, named the "SteelLord," married a human woman from Earth. She gave birth to The Stehle family, creating the world's first superhumans. As the family grew, they recruited other superhuman allies to join their cause in protecting Earth from cataclysmic threats and evil. This ended up evolving into the superhero team, The Protectors.
Zach

Sounds pretty simple.
Josh

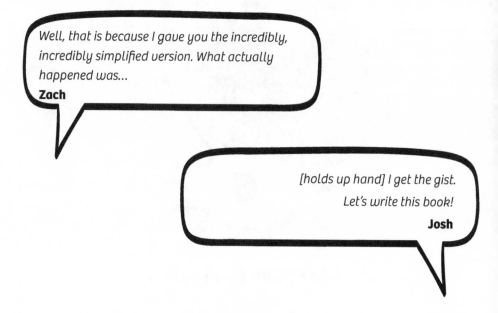

Well, that is because I gave you the incredibly, incredibly simplified version. What actually happened was...
Zach

[holds up hand] I get the gist. Let's write this book!
Josh

We have all seen the viral videos.

Videos of Stephen Wiltshire, who, after a twenty-minute flight over the city of Tokyo, was able to draw a thirty-three-foot-long detailed portrait of the city, including every building, bridge, road, car, stoplight, and landmark in sight, purely from memory.

Videos of Kim Peek, who can read books two pages at once, in roughly three seconds, and remember everything that he read.

Videos of Daniel Tammet, who can recite pi to the 22,514th decimal, over five hours and with perfect accuracy.

Humans should not be able to do these things. Humans are not able to do these things. Yet some great minds CAN do them. These indescribable and unimaginable acts of the human brain, that many would deem impossible, have been accomplished by a select few individuals who push the boundaries of what the mind is capable of accomplishing. To most, these skills are uncanny, and even alien-like. The uninformed may call them magic. But we, the psychologists, thinkers, and learners, we call it...

"The savant syndrome."

ALRIGHT, THAT'S ENOUGH OF THE FLOWERY language, ninth grade Josh.

What you just read was the opening section of a psychology paper I wrote back in high school when I was fourteen or fifteen. After turning in that paper, I remember thinking that I was so brilliant, and everybody else in my class just didn't understand how to write like I did.

That was years ago. Now that I've had some time to reflect, I've concluded that I shouldn't trust the distorted memory of the guy who would walk around high school with his shoes untied, thinking that it would "make him look cooler to the ladies." I now realize that the only thing my untied shoes did for me was make me trip on the staircases. It was not a good look for the captain of the school's basketball team.

However, I do think that there were some redeeming qualities about the opening of that paper. Perhaps not the excessive language, but the message behind it.

Throughout the world, some people possess extraordinary mental gifts, some of which classify under the umbrella of "savant syndrome." Oftentimes, people with savant syndrome, referred to as "savants," also have autism. However, there have been recorded cases of non-autistic people gaining savant-like abilities after receiving a brain alteration of some sort. A popular example of this is a man named Orlando Serrell. Born in 1968, Orlando was not autistic or brain-damaged, but he developed the unique ability of calendar calculating after he was struck on the left side of the head by a baseball. The day after that baseball game, he noticed he was able to tell which day of the week any calendar day had fallen on. He could even recall what the weather had been on that specific day. This phenomenon is known as "acquired savant syndrome," and it continues to be documented to this day.

However, savant syndrome is documented mostly within the autism community. Of course, not many individuals with ASD have savant-like skills. True savants are not only incredibly rare but also often representational of the greatest possible extremes in cognitive ability. For example, Stephen Wiltshire, the guy who drew a thirty-three-foot portrait of Tokyo after a twenty-minute viewing session, is also completely mute. Kim Peek, who can read entire books in literal seconds, has trouble walking and speaking. And Daniel Tammet, who can recite pi to the 22,514th decimal... actually, that guy is incredibly brilliant. He is also capable of learning languages at an unprecedented rate, and he even taught himself to speak fluent Icelandic in less than a week, just for fun. Good for him!

Still, savant syndrome is so rare that many people would deem it inconsequential. So why, as a community, should we care about it? Well, even though the condition itself is rare, savant-like tendencies and behaviors can still be seen in some autistic people. Examples of these include a person possessing an extreme interest in one or a few things with difficulty engaging in other activities or a person being incredibly gifted at a certain skill while struggling with skills most neurotypical people would consider to be standard. Think about Zach's knack for remembering superheroes despite struggling to remember the letters of the alphabet, recalling friends' names, or driving to a location he's been to a thousand times.

These are tendencies found in savants that are also present in the autistic community. Therefore, the better we understand how autism affects the brain, including savant syndrome, the better we can provide care and service for people with cognitive disabilities. This must be a community effort!

Some of the abilities that these savants have would absolutely blow the socks right off your feet. In fact, I've purposely left a few famous examples out of this book for you to find. If you're a fan of insane musical ability, uncanny memory skills, or other unbelievable abilities, then do a quick Google search. It is absolutely worth the effort.

In the meantime, here is a bit of information that you'll never find on the Internet. Well, until this book is published, at least. Prepare yourself for the hottest take of your lifetime...

Zach is a savant.

Are you surprised? Did you see it coming? Do I sound excited to write about this? (I am.)

Zach is a savant, though it isn't in the way most people would picture it. Zach has absolutely no spatial recognition and is therefore a terrible artist. He has no musical ability and barely ever listens to music, except for the three or four songs he hears while watching superhero videos on YouTube. He has virtually no athletic ability (and his reflexes are duller than the spoon he uses to feed his cat). But his mind, in some specific respects, is brilliant.

Like many savants, Zach's first flashes of brilliance began at an early age. My mom loves to tell the story of how he taught himself to read. Yes, you read that correctly. Despite his numerous developmental delays, including verbal communication, fine motor skills, and auditory processing, Zach taught himself to read and was binging through *Harry Potter* and *Star Wars* novels while the other kids his age were still learning that l-m-n-o-p are five different letters and not just one big letter. For the record, Zach didn't know this either, but it never seemed to affect his ability to read.

Zach showed signs of autism at an early age, so when my parents took him to neuropsychologists, he left many of them completely dumbfounded.

My mom tells this next story the best, so imagine me narrating this in a mom-like voice:

———

Mom:
"There was this one neuropsychologist who just did not believe us. We were at his first appointment with her, and Zach had his nose in a *Star Wars* book. Not a kid's book... one of those novel-type, five-hundred-page books with no pictures. Remember, Zach was around five at the time, and he was *reading* the full novel.

'He's just looking at the words!' The neuropsychologist insisted at least three times, and we were getting frustrated. We needed her to understand that our child was not "just developmentally delayed," or PDD-NOS as the doctors liked to label him (Pervasive Developmental Disorder – Not Otherwise Specified). Finally, we took the book from Zach and closed it shut. We handed it to the neuropsychologist and told her to pick out any part of the book. Zach watched her, half listening but completely focused on the book he wanted back in his possession. The neuropsychologist sighed, turned her back so that Zach couldn't see her, and flipped to the page where Darth Vader cut off Luke Skywalker's hand. She read one line and closed it with a snap before handing it back to Zach. Immediately, Zach opened the book, flipped to the part that she was just reading, and pointed to the exact line she had just said aloud."

Josh:
"Awesome. She must have been shocked! That story is going to be great for my book."

Mom:
"Anything for my favorite child. You're so much smarter and cooler than your sister, by the way."

———

Okay, my mom didn't actually say that last part, but the rest of the story is true. Zach has always been a brilliant reader! I do understand why so many people, even specialists in the field of neuropsychology, have doubted his ability, though. Like some people with autism (but not all), Zach does not enjoy the feeling of suspense. He prefers to experience his stories when he knows exactly what's going to happen at the end. So, Zach doesn't read from the beginning of a new book. Instead, he begins by reading the very last page, then skips to someplace in the middle, then skips to somewhere else, and on and on, until the whole book is completed. Then, he pieces the book's story, plot, and characters together in his head. To this day, this is still how Zach enjoys reading stories.

This unique personality trait alone is a critical component in Zach's insane comic book knowledge. Zach reads the same superhero stories over and over again, each time enjoying the story just as much as the first read through. When he doesn't understand a plot point or recognize a character, he must research that mystery until he knows everything possible, or else he will not be able to enjoy the story. It is through these countless comic book rereads and Wikipedia searches over the last two decades that Zach has developed his incredible wealth of superhero knowledge.

Of course, right now you're probably thinking, "but many people like to read and research. That isn't the sign of a savant!"

And to that I say, "Good catch, eagle-eyed reader!"

You're right. Zach is not a savant-like reader, but his reading and researching prowess is what led him to his great passion. **For Zach, reading and researching are simply the gateways to creating.**

Remember in chapter 4 when we talked about Zach's innate skill of remembering everything there was possibly to know about superheroes? Well, that skill is about to come in handy. Allow me to introduce you to Zach's very own, completely original superhero team:

The Protectors

Active Members:

1. (X)(E)**Zach Stehle**()(leader, founding member, senior member, council member, field support, history support, tactical support)(Powers: Master tactician, stealth expert, weapon expert, and martial artist)

2. (X)(S)*Eric Stehle**()(senior member, founding member, council member, field support, tactical support, business support)(Powers: Ice and snow manipulation, master tactician, businessman, and martial artist)

3. (X)(E)**Josh Stehle***()(senior member, founding member, council member, third in command, head of the Protectors' engineering/mechanical/inventing department, field support, tech support, demolitions expert, pilot, engineer)(Powers: Luck manipulation, master archer, stealth expert, driver, inventor, pilot, skilled martial artist, and gadget user)

4. (X)(S)*Cheryl Stehle**()(senior member, founding member, council member, field support)(Powers: Telepathy, telekinesis, and expert martial artist)

5. (X)(E)*Becca Stehle*()(third in command, senior member, founding member, council member, field support, tactical support, magic support, political support)(Powers: Water manipulation, underwater adaptation, superhuman condition, magic user, master tactician, weapon expert, and martial artist)

6. (E)<u>Doctor Jim Roman</u>*()(second in command, senior member, founding member, council member, head of the Protector's science/forensic/medical department, field support, tech support, scientist)(Powers: Advanced armored suit provided superhuman condition, energy manipulation, flight, built-in weapons and gadgets, survival adaptation, tech control, master tactician, scientist, hacker, inventor, and skilled martial artist)

7. (X)(S)**Tom Ford***()(senior member, founding member, council member, field support, tech support)(Powers: Teleportation, expert tactician, stealth expert, computer hacker, and martial artist)

8. (X)(E)*Ethan Argon*()(senior member, founding member, council member, field support, magic support, medical support)(Powers: magic user, skilled martial artist, and medic)

9. (S)*Nazir Khan/Stormknight**()(senior member, founding member, council member, field support)(Powers: Weather manipulation, flight, and expert martial artist)

10. (X)(S)<u>Erin Hines/Moon Mage</u>*()(senior member, founding member, council member, field support, magic support)(Powers: Lunar magic-user both without and through the Lance of Luna, superhuman condition, master martial artist, and weapon expert)

11. (E)*Horus**()(senior member, founding member, council member, field support, history support, head of the Protectors' tactical/operations/reconnaissance department)(Powers: Heliopolis God physiology, flight, superhuman condition, master tactician, weapon expert, and martial artist)

12. (S)<u>Prince Vic'Tor</u>*()(senior member, founding member, council member, advisor on alien customs, field support, tactical support, political support)(Powers: Starian physiology, superhuman condition, light manipulation, size manipulation, flight, and expert martial artist)

13. (E)**Carol Wilson/Supervisor***()(senior member, founding member, council member, tech support, tactical support, mission controller, communications, head of the Protectors' IT/Technician/Maintenance department)(Powers: Master tactician, detective, and hacker)

14. (X)(E)<u>Albert</u>*()(senior member, scientist, council member, medical support, tech support)(Powers: Ape physiology, superhuman condition, master inventor, scientist, and skilled martial artist)

15. (E)*General Isaac McWilliams/General Power**()(senior member, council member, field support, tactical support, military liaison)(Powers: Power manipulation and projection, superhuman condition, master tactician, and martial artist)

16. (S)<u>Salvation</u>()(senior member, field support, tactical support, tech support, forensics, pilot)(Powers: Robot physiology, superhuman condition, energy manipulation, built-in weapons and gadgets, tech control, master tactician, hacker, martial artist, and marksman)

17. (E)**James Redfeather/Swift***()(senior member, field support)(Powers: Superspeed, kinetic energy absorption, enhanced durability, and expert martial artist)

18. (S)*Dominion**()(senior member, field support, advisor on alien customs, tactical support, political support)(Powers: Apexian physiology, superhuman condition, expert weapon expert, tactician, and martial artist)

19. (E)*Doctor Patrick Wildblaze/Dinoman*()(senior member, field support, scientist)(Powers: Dino physiology, superhuman condition, flight, tail and claws, expert martial artist, and scientist)

20. (E)**Digger Duster/The Mole**()(senior member, field support)(Powers: Mole physiology, superhuman condition, can dig through stone, concrete, metal, etc. sharp claws, enhanced senses though blind, and skilled martial artist)

21. (E)*Queen Ayo/Ashe Oba(Spirit Ruler)**()(senior member, field support, magic support, political support)(Powers: Ancient Magic user, beast controller and summoner, animal power user, spiritual manipulation, plant manipulation, master tactician, weapon expert, tracker, and martial artist)

22. (S)<u>Yang Wu/Sun Sorcerer</u>*()(senior member, field support, magic support)(Powers: Solar magic-user both without and through the Staff of Solus, superhuman condition, skilled martial artist, and weapon expert)

23. (S)**Carmitta***()(senior member, tech support)(Powers: AI physiology)

24. (E)**Ballar**()(senior member, field support, magic support)(Powers: Druid physiology, plant manipulation, and animal connection)

25. (E)**Hephaestus***(20,22,27)(senior member, tech support, engineer, mechanic)(Powers: Olympian God physiology, superhuman condition, fire manipulation, master inventor, engineer, and mechanic)

26. (E)**Master Tenzin***()(field support, senior member)(Powers: Spiritual communication, healing, master martial artist, stealth expert, weapons expert, and chief)

27. (S)<u>Barret Pike/Time Watcher</u>*()(field support, senior member)(Powers: Advanced battle suit user with advanced weapons, gadgets, and time travel, skilled martial artist, marksman, pilot, temporal agent, and mechanic)

28. (X)(S)*Hercules**()(senior member, field support)(Powers: Olympian Demigod physiology, superhuman condition, master weapon expert, and martial artist)

29. (E)<u>Layla</u>*()(field support, magic support)(Powers: Angel physiology, superhuman condition, flight, angel and light magic user, expert martial artist, weapon expert, and tactician)

30. (X)(E)<u>Captain Franklin Hawkins/Skyblaze</u>*(14,24)(senior member, field support, pilot)(Powers: Armored flight suit equipped with jetpack, survival adaptation, gadgets, and weapons, expert tactician, pilot, and martial artist)

31. (E)<u>Scrappy</u>*()(tech support, mechanic)(Powers: Robot physiology, master hacker, and mechanic)

32. (E)**Doctor Henry "Hank" Maxwell/Supergenius***()(tech support, medic, scientist, inventor, engineer, forensics) (Powers: Gadget user, expert driver, scientist, inventor, detective, hacker, and skilled martial artist)

33. (E)<u>Jordan Hellson/Doctor Demon</u>*()(field support, magic support)(Powers: Bounded to the demon, Nullfiend, superhuman condition, flight, demon magic and dark magic user, skilled martial artist, tactician, and weapon expert)

34. (E)<u>Ted Howard/Captain Liberty</u>*()(field support)(Powers: Torch of Liberty provided Superhuman condition, energy manipulation, survival adaptation, flight, dimensional travel, and skilled martial artist)

35. (E)*Arnold Pendragon/Iron Knight**()(field support, tech support, magic support, history support)(Powers: Advanced armored suit, superhuman condition, built-in weapons, survival adaptation, magic sword, tech-based shield, skilled martial artist, marksman, and weapon expert)

36. (E)*Merlin**()(field support, history support, magic support)(Powers: Magic-user)

37. (E)*Whitehorn the Unicorn**()(field support, magic support) (Powers: Unicorn physiology, unicorn magic user)

38. (X)(S)**Noah Wilson/Boomerang Man***()(field support, tech support, inventor, demolitions expert)(Powers: Expert stealth expert, marksman, inventor, thief, martial artist, and weaponized boomerangs)

39. (S)<u>Tone'Lord-Armd</u>*()(field support, advisor on alien customs, tactical support, political support)(Powers:

Martian physiology, superhuman condition, advanced Martian gadgets, expert tactician, martial artist, marksman, and pilot)

40. (S)<u>Dual'Tral-Armd</u>*()(field support, tech support, mechanic, engineer, pilot)(Powers: Martian physiology, superhuman condition, four arms, skilled martial artist, expert mechanic, engineer, and pilot)

41. (E)<u>Sara Archer/Guardian</u>*()(field support)(Powers: Superhuman condition, energy manipulation, flight, survival adaptations, force field generation, dimensional travel, expert martial artist, and markswoman)

42. (E)<u>Obsidian the Gargoyle</u>*()(field support, tracker) (Powers: Gargoyle physiology, master weapon expert, and martial artist)

43. (S)<u>Doctor Anton Kurpin/Gravity Man</u>*()(field support, scientist)(Powers: Gravity manipulation and expert scientist)

44. (X)(S)<u>Ember</u>()(field support, magic support)(Powers: Dragon physiology, flight, superhuman condition, fire breath, portal creation, and survival adaptation)

45. (X)(S)*Palin Silvershield**()(field support, magic support, medic)(Powers: Lightforge physiology, mystical shield allowing light manipulation, healing, teleportation, master weapon expert, and martial artist)

46. (S)<u>Dracula</u>()(field support, magic support, history support, tactical support)(Powers: Vampire physiology, magic user, shape-shifting, flight, darkness manipulation, master tactician, stealth expert, weapon expert, and martial artist)

47. (S)*Simon Gajewski/Boombox*()(field support, pilot)(Powers: Sound manipulation, expert marksman, pilot, and martial artist)

48. (S)*Diego Morales/Killer Shell*()(field support, tech support, engineer, mechanic)(Powers: Advanced turtle-based suit

with built-in weapons and gadgets, skilled inventor, and martial artist)

49. (S)*Scáthach**(field support)(Powers: God physiology, superhuman condition, master martial artist, stealth expert, weapons expert, and tactician)

50. (S)*Avik Patel/Rubber Man**()(field support)(Powers: Elasticity, shape-shifting, expert martial artist)

51. (X)(S)*Hu*(field support)(Powers: Dragon physiology, flight, superhuman condition, water breath, portal creation, and survival adaptation)

52. (E)*Colonel Viktor Lenkov/Crimson Rocket**()(field support, tech support, mechanic, military liaison)(Powers: Advanced suit equipped with a jetpack, built in weapons and gadgets, superhuman condition, survival adaptation, expert martial artist, marksman, pilot, and mechanic)

53. (S)*Risu**()(field support, tech support, demolitions expert)(Powers: Anthropometric squirrel physiology, flight via jetpack, skilled martial artist, weapon expert, archery, and stealth expert)

54. (S)*Luthor Sanders/Techboard**()(field support, tech support)(Powers: Weaponized surfboard with flight, gravity manipulation, and magnetic attachments, weaponized suit, skilled martial artist, pilot, marksman, mechanic, and inventor)

55. (S)*Sofia Lupin/Lupa**()(field support, tracker)(Powers: Werewolf physiology, superhuman condition, expert martial artist, stealth expert, and tracker)

56. (S)<u>Sun Wukung/Monkey King</u>*()(field support)(Powers: God physiology, superhuman condition, cloud creation, shape-shifting, master martial artist, and weapon expert)

57. (S)*Ka'Boom*()(field support)(Powers: Bomborge physiology, superhuman condition, explosion manipulation, and skilled martial artist)

58. (E)**Pharaoh Atum-Ra***()(field support, political support, magic support)(Powers: Mummy physiology, elasticity, magic user)

59. (E)**Webs***()(field support)(Powers: Giant spider physiology, web shooting, wall-climbing, poisoned fangs, and stealth expert)

60. (E)*Piper*()(field support)(Powers: Hairians physiology, Prehensile hair, hair shape-shifting, expert martial artist, and stealth expert)

61. (S)*Dr. Tiliy Flamel/The Alchemist*()(field support, magic support, scientist)(Powers: Alchemy, matter manipulation, skilled doctor, scientist, and medic)

62. (E)**Agent Leto Drakos/Shapechanger***()(field support)(Powers: Shapeshifting, expert martial artist, weapon expert, markswoman, stealth expert, hacker, pilot, and driver)

63. (E)*Magamolem**()(field support)(Powers: Magravel physiology, superhuman condition, fire and magma manipulation, and shape-shifting)

64. (X)(E)*Cyger*()(field support, tracker)(Powers: Cybernetic tiger with advanced weapons and gadgets)

65. (X)(S)*Dominic Woods/Sniper**()(field support)(Powers: Enhanced senses, jetpack user, master marksman, stealth expert, and skilled martial artist)

66. (E)*Chiron**()(field support, tactical support, trainer)(Powers: Centaur physiology, master weapons expert, tactician, martial artist, healer, and archer)

67. (E)**Agent Wilfred Suit***()(field support, liaison)(Powers: Use weaponized suits, master martial artist, marksman, stealth expert, tactician, driver, pilot, and hacker)

68. (E)*Zoey Vector/Mosquito**()(field support)(Powers: Flight, size changing, stingers, and energy projection)

69. (S)**Evan Quills/Thorn***()(field support)(Powers: Half-Spiklor physiology, spike growth and shooting, adjusting them to heat up, grow sharper or longer, and freeze, expert marksman, stealth expert, and martial artist)

70. (E)*Doctor Elias McCorn/Professor Size**()(field support, scientist)(Powers: Advanced suit allowing for size manipulation, master scientist, and skilled martial artist)

71. (E)*Sharkous**()(field support, tracker)(Powers: Atlantean Shark physiology, superhuman condition, underwater breathing and adaption, skilled tracker, and martial artist)

72. (E)**Thunderwing**()(field support)(Powers: Griffin physiology, superhuman condition, and flight)

73. (E)**Bast***()(field support, tracker)(Powers: Heliopolis God physiology, superhuman condition, master martial artist, weapon expert, tracker, and stealth expert)

74. (X)(S)*Targath the Unwise**()(field support)(Powers: Superhuman condition, expert weapons expert, and skilled martial artist)

75. (S)*Ruby Shade/Time Witch**()field support, history support, magic support, medical support)(Powers: Time manipulation, healing, dimensional travel, and sand manipulation)

76. (X)(E)*Aka Mariko/Red Samurai**()(field support, magic support)(Powers: Mystic Sword providing energy manipulation, ancestors communications, master martial artist, and weapon expert)

77. (X)(S)**Jack Patch/Jack of Diamonds***()(field support, tech support, demolitions expert)(Powers: Grappling hooks and weaponized trick cards user, expert tactician, driver, stealth expert, marksman, inventor, thief, hacker, martial artist, and gadget user)

78. (S)**Martin Kekoa/Elemental Blaster**()(field support, driver, pilot)(Powers: Have a blaster that can release the

elements including wind, earth, water, ice, fire, electricity, etc., master marksman, skilled martial artist, pilot, driver, and stealth expert)

79. (S)*Grant Williamson/The Bard**()(field support)(Powers: Magical harp, reality and sound manipulation, and skilled martial artist)

80. (S)<u>Sean McGuire/Ghosthawk</u>*()(field support)(Powers: Flight, phasing, clawed talons, expert martial artist)

81. (E)<u>Peter Lockheart/Awesome Man</u>*()(field support) (Powers: Connection to the Awesome Force allowing for superhuman condition, energy projection, survival adaptation, flight, and expert martial artist)

82. (E)**Agent George Hardy/Shades**()(field support)(Powers: Weaponized glasses, master spy, martial artist, tactician, driver, and pilot)

83. (E)**Kevin Fox/Night Striker***()(field support, tech support, spy, interrogator, forensics)(Powers: shadow jumping, expert martial artist, weapon expert, marksman, stealth expert, hacker, detective, and tactician)

84. (S)*Dr. Scott Greenwood/Medio*()(field medic, tech support) (Powers: Cyborg physiology and medical technology built-in force field generator)

85. (E)*Sobek**()(field support)(Powers: Heliopolis God physiology, water manipulation, animal manipulation, superhuman condition, master martial artist, and weapon expert)

86. (E)*Nekhbet*()(field support)(Powers: Heliopolis God physiology, flight, superhuman condition, enhanced senses, master martial artist, and weapon expert)

87. (E)*Fey*()(field support, magic support, healer)(Powers: Asgardian God physiology, superhuman condition, limited temperature and earth manipulation, magic user, healing, master martial artist, and weapon expert)

88. (S)*Ares**()(field support, tactical support)(Powers: Olympian God physiology, superhuman condition, war manipulation, limited death manipulation, weapon summoning, master martial artist, weapon expert, and tactician)

89. (E)*Hecate**()(field support, magic support)(Powers: Olympian Titan physiology, superhuman condition, magic user, death control, seer, and master tactician)

90. (E)*Robert McShield/Guardian**()(field support)(Powers: Superhuman condition, energy manipulation, flight, survival adaptations, force field generation, dimensional travel, expert martial artist, and marksman)

91. (E)*Jamie Shaw/Black Wolf**()(field support, tactical support, tech support)(Powers: Superhuman condition, gadget user, master artist, marksman, tactician, stealth expert, and inventor)

92. (S)*Mali Knight/Black Gem**()(field support, magic support)(Powers: Black gem, or the Gem of Umbra providing force field generation, superhuman condition, energy projection, flight, magic manipulation, and skilled martial artist)

93. (E)*Tabbith Arms/Weaponzier**()(field support)(Access to a pocket dimension with any weapon she desires, master martial artist, weapon expert, markswoman, and stealth expert)

94. (S)<u>Xbrain</u>*()(tech support, scientist)(Powers: Overbrain physiology, cyborg physiology, telepathy, telekinesis, built-in weapons and gadgets, and master scientist)

95. (S)<u>Luz Reyes/*Defender*</u>*()(field support)(Powers: Symbiote physiology, shapeshifting, built-in weapons, survival adaptations)

96. (E)**Lucius Flame/Phoenix**()(field support, council member)(Powers: Fire manipulation, flight, master martial artist, and tactician)

97. (S)**Victor Jackson/Overshock***()(field support)(Powers: Electricity manipulation, flight, magnetism, force field generation, and skilled martial artist)

98. (E)**Coilius***()(field support)(Powers: Sperentia physiology, superhuman condition, flexibility, claws on hands, venom manipulation, and expert martial artist)

99. (S)_**Azra Ayad/Glyph**_()(field support, magic support) (Powers: Glyphs-caster with different effects such as portals, elements projections, and structures, and skilled martial artist)

100. (S)_Professor Merra Shaan/Techchair_()(field support, tech support, scientist)(Powers: Advanced hover chair with advanced weapons and gadgets, expert scientist, and inventor)

101. (E)**Dr. Severus Lopez/Potioneer***()(field support, scientist)(Powers: Potions that give different effects and skilled scientist)

102. (E)_Kameron Parks/Guardian_(field support)(Powers: Force field generation, giving them different effects such as energy projection, flight, superhuman condition, and master martial artist)

103. (S)_Mangi_*(field support)(Powers: Asgardian Demigod physiology, superhuman condition, lighting manipulation, master martial artist, and weapon expert)(Sword)

104. (S)_Modi_*(field support)(Powers: Asgardian Demigod physiology, superhuman condition, lighting manipulation, master martial artist, and weapon expert)(Ax and shield)

105. (E)_Kevin Shade/Maskman_*()(field support, magic support) (Powers: Various masks that provide different powers)

106. (S)**Josh Erikson/Captain All-Star***()(field support) (Powers: Superhuman condition, can summon weapons from his golf bag, master weapon expert and martial artist)

107. (E)**Polly McCoy/Shape Arrow***()(field support)(Powers: Magic bow- user, turning her arrows into anything she wants such as animals, structures, and objects, master marksman, stealth expert, and tracker, and skilled martial artist)

108. (E)**Ivanger Stormshield/Stormsrker***()(field support) (Powers: Demigod physiology, superhuman condition, magic ax with lighting manipulation, master martial artist, and weapon expert)

109. (S)*Richard McCowern/The Lance*()(field support, magic support)(Powers: Magic lance with release energy, skilled marksman, and martial artist)

110. (S)*Ghost Tank*()(field support)(Powers: Living tank)

111. (E)*Cu'be*()(field support, tech support)(Hexahedron physiology, superhuman intelligence, technology hacking, energy projection, and teleportation)

112. (S)Core()(field support)(Planetoid psychology, superhuman condition, earth manipulation, telepathy, and telekinesis)

113. (S)Sasha Divine*()(field support)(Powers: Divine physiology, superhuman condition, energy manipulation and projection, and connection to the Earth)

114. (E)*Mimir**()(tactical support)(Powers: Asgardian God physiology, Superhuman intelligence, and master tactician)

115. (S)Ash*()(field support, tactical support, demolitions expert, pilot)(Powers: Wartiles physiology, underwater adaptation, invisibility, expert tactician, stealth expert, marksman, weapon expert, and martial artist)

Yes, I'm sure you simply skimmed that entire list, just like I did when I copied and pasted it into my book. Lucky for you, I have spent years discussing these superheroes in depth with my brother, so here is a rundown of what I have learned:

The Avengers have fifteen active members. Meanwhile, Zach's superhero team, the Protectors, has *one hundred and fifteen.* For each of these characters, Zach has created a unique backstory, powers, aliases, complex narrative arcs, personal dramas between them and the other characters, and dozens and dozens of interconnected stories. Zach knows how every single one of those characters thinks and feels about every other character. He has written complex, multiple-page stories for every one of them. Oh, and don't ask me what the asterisks, bolded words, or letters in parentheses mean. I pulled this list from one of Zach's several, incredibly complex "The Protectors" Google Docs (so, basically, I have no idea).

Wait, I almost forgot! Listed above are just the active members! Of course, what is a superhero team without their support staff, advisors, and reserve? Don't worry, Zach has a list for them too:

- Nora Allison (lawyer, public relations advisor)
- Logan Martin (lawyer)
- Wanda Nest (personal aide to Commander Zach Stehle)
- Bob (air control chief)
- Tomas Blade (UN liaison, political advisor)
- Hector Jeeves (head of staff)
- Doctor Mary Thomas (therapist)
- Aquafish (pilot)
- Lagon (operative)
- Bill (engineer/mechanic)
- Matthew (operative)
- Nick (orderly)
- Juan (driver)
- Howard (operative)
- Bobby (maintenance)
- Sam (engineer)
- Wing (pilot)

- Scales (operative)
- Greenwood (operative)
- Harold (field medic)
- Bill Morgan (operative)
- Aadesh (head of the Monastery)
- Jugger (technician)
- Aput (head of the Glacier)
- Johnson (driver, operative)
- Thompson (operative, pilot, technician)
- Li Wung (operative, head of the Chinese base of operations)
- Chang Wung (operative)
- Dr. Li Chan (medic)
- Ben (driver)
- Morse (pilot)
- Morgan (medic)
- Marshall (engineer)
- Morrow (operative, driver)
- Chase (operative)
- Oborak (operative)
- Wood (operative)
- Kim (head chief)
- Blade (operative)
- De Mavis (operative)
- Green (driver)
- Foxglow (operative)
- Enzo (Head of the French Outpost)
- Bellatrix (operative, field medic)
- Maxwell (engineer)
- Fox (operative, pilot)
- Mack (owner of Mack's, operative)
- Daren (bartender at Mack's, operative)
- Hugo (bartender at Mack's, operative)
- Cody (operative)
- Flare (Second in Command of Ash's Warlounge, operative)
- Dr. Cord (doctor, field medic)
- Dr. Alexander Meda (medical doctor)

- Harrison (pilot)

Numerous unnamed operatives, janitors, chefs, pilots, drivers, engineers, mechanics, doctors, nurses, and orderlies from humans and Warlounge members

In case you *also* skimmed this list instead of learning every member of The Protectors' support staff, just know that Hugo is a bartender at the superhero team's personal club, Mack's (yes, Zach is very in-depth), and he makes a wicked strawberry margarita. This is canon.

Once again, each of these characters is fully fleshed out, with connecting storylines, complex moral compasses, skills, and weaknesses. But here is the kicker:

This is just one of Zach's superhero teams.

In fact, he has about a dozen, all expanded out to this scale and magnitude. Then, of course, he has created just as many villains who all work together to stop these heroes in a variety of complex, interesting, and utterly creative ways.

Of course, Zach doesn't limit himself to just superheroes on Earth. His homebrew universe extends to planets far outside the Milky Way Galaxy, complete with dozens of unique alien races, interplanetary and open space combat encounters, incredibly complex political relations between morally distrusting alien races, and lots and lots of Google Docs.

He writes everything down. He has thousands of pages, all listing unique stories of his prized characters and their epic battles against evil. In his free time at home or on his break at the grocery store, Zach strides around in his own little world, bringing his universe to life, while being completely oblivious to the real world around him. He doesn't go a day without creating a new story in his head, and he always writes it down in a Google Doc. Most amazingly, he never forgets a single story he comes up with.

At least, that is what he's always said. For years, I didn't believe him because how could I believe such a ludicrous claim? There was no way that Zach could ever remember all one hundred and fifteen members of The Protectors off the top of his head and without even a minute to think! Impossible, I say, impossible! (Insert obvious foreshadowing here.)

Then one day, when I was helping Zach practice highway driving, I decided to put my brother to the test. At the time, I was sitting in the passenger seat and scrolling through his massive list of The Protectors members.

Then, at the worst possible moment since Zach was preparing to merge into a new lane of traffic, I said, "Okay, bro. Name all one hundred and fifteen of The Protectors. Go."

"Josh, I'm driving." That was Zach's classic response when he was agitated while behind the wheel. Of course, I understood why. He didn't like driving on highways due to the unpredictability of the other cars, but what kind of brother was I if I didn't instigate a little?

"Nahhh. Come on. I bet you a nickel that you can't!"

"No."

Silence ensued. I glanced back at the Google Doc, my suspicions having been proven true. Of course, Zach couldn't name all one hundred and fifteen of The Protectors. This guy was all talk and no action!

"You're all talk and no action!" I exclaimed as we approached a stop sign. Once our car was completely still, Zach looked at me seriously.

"If I do this," he said, "then you don't tell Mom and Dad that I was distracted while I was driving."

"Hmmmmm." I pretended to stroke my chin in thought. "Okay! I won't!"

"You promise?"

"I promise."

Zach took a deep breath. "Zach Stehle, Eric Stehle, Josh Stehle, Cheryl Stehle, Becca Stehle, Dr. Jim Roman, Tom Ford, Ethan Argon, Nazir Khan also known as Stormknight, Erin Hines, Horus, Prince Vic'Tor..."

Zach recited all one hundred and fifteen active members, all at once, without skipping a beat or skipping a member of the team. By the time he was done, I was so shocked I sat the rest of the car ride in silence. Zach, on the other hand, was quite pleased with himself and even drove a few digits over the speed limit.

I think back to that memory fondly. I'm glad Zach can remember everything he has come up with for his superhero universe. For one thing, the amount of content Zach has created, through both characters and storylines, rivals both the Marvel and DC universes in scale. This is a fact, proven with numbers and stuff. (Trust me. There are Google Docs.)

Perhaps the greatest part of Zach's superhero universe isn't the scale of it at all. In truth, I believe it is the people he puts into his worlds that make them truly special. Maybe you have already noticed this, but not all of Zach's Protectors are completely fictional characters. In addition to his original heroes, Zach also takes the most important people in his life from the real world, gives each of them powers, abilities, nicknames, and an incredibly detailed backstory, and includes them in his Protectors universe. Everybody in my family is a founding member of the Protectors team. Zach is a combat expert, full of cunning strategy and stealth. Our dad has the powers of snow and ice manipulation and is a master tactician. Our sister, Becca, can waterbend better than the Avatar ever could, and our mom has the power of telekinesis. Even Sean McGuire, code name Ghosthawk, is number eighty on the active members list.

Then there's me, Superhero Josh Stehle. Zach has characterized me as a billionaire playboy who loves to pull pranks on his brother. Protector Josh Stehle is a funny, comic relief character who goes on duo adventures with his best friend and oftentimes stumbles into saving the day. I think the description fits me perfectly.

But, of course, it was Zach who had the last laugh. For he did not give me any superpowers, oh no...

After all my excessive trash talking about how Hawkeye is the lamest Avenger of them all, the only weapon I was given in the Protectors universe was...

You guessed it, a bow and arrow.

The Protectors: Generations

The following is an original story by Zach and me. The story takes place in the Protectors Universe and occurs in the "Generations" alternate timeline. In this story, the year is 2097, and the Protectors superhero team has been retired for many years. Over a decade has passed since the world was in crisis, and, with the advent of advanced military technology, the Earth's governments have decided that the planet no longer needs the Protectors on active duty. While most of the team have moved on from their crime-fighting days, embracing their fame as celebrities or retiring to a life of peace, some have continued the battle against evil, operating in secret and protecting the world from the never-ending threats of the Universe!

This is a co-authored piece. Zach writes most of the rough drafts for each chapter while I write the final versions. Please note that the story, plot, and characters are all completely Zach's creations. It is our goal to one day finish and publish this book or rather series of books. However, the following chapter is a rough draft and is subject to change before its final release.

The Protectors: Generations

The New Dawn
By: The Stehle Bros

Chapter 1

"ERGH..." ZACH STEEL GRUNTS IN PAIN WHILE
yet another dirty rag is soaked with his blood.

The fabled Protector is standing in the bathroom of his New York City penthouse, covered in bruises, cuts, and scars, and is trying desperately to stop the bleeding from the gash across his forehead. On the counter next to him, the bloody rags have piled higher than the tops of the faucets, and the sink water has turned bright red. Zach glances back into the mirror, his eye twitching in annoyance as the blood continues to flow from the gash.

The day did not go as planned.

What began as a routine crime watch evolved so quickly into a phenomenon he couldn't explain. What was the Umbra Clan crime syndicate doing at that abandoned warehouse? Who was controlling them, and how were they so powerful in combat? Zach had never fought thugs who possessed such an understanding of energy manipulation before.

The veteran superhero shakes his head. Umbra Clan must have been gaining that immense power from someone or something. But Zach knows one thing for certain. He must get to the bottom of it, before they put New York City, and potentially the world, in even more danger.

Zach dabs his forehead one last time with a rag, before throwing the bloody pile into the garbage. That will have to do.

Knock, knock, knock!

Zach looks up in surprise as the door to the bathroom rattles.

"Hello? Who's in there? I've got to get in there!" a voice calls out from outside the door.

"Occupied!" Zach yells back, rolling his eyes as the door opens anyway. "What's the point of asking if you're going to walk in regardless?"

"Formality," Josh Steel says with a grin. "I just need to wash up really quickly. Brittney is coming over and I want to... WOAH! What happened to you?!"

"Just... work."

"Work. Right." Josh nods several times. "Even though we are both retired and have been since we saved the entire world, you know, many years ago.... Got it."

Zach nods. "Correct. Now if you'll excuse me..." He tries to walk past Josh, but the retired Protector does not let him pass.

"Not so fast. Where do you think you are going?"

"Back to work. There's something I have to fix."

"Zach." Josh leans casually against the bloody sink. "You are one of, if not, the greatest hero in the history of mankind. Don't you think it's okay to take a day off? No, better yet, the rest of your life off? The fight is over. We won! Earth doesn't need us anymore, but do you know who does need us?" He pauses for dramatic effect. "Brittney! Look, bro, let's take it easy tonight. You and me!"

Zach shakes his head. "I'm sorry, Josh, but I can't. Something was wrong today, really wrong. I can't explain it."

Josh chuckles to himself. "What is it? Did a guy rob a convenience store? No, no, no, let me guess. It was the Umbra Clan! They stole a hot dog from a street vendor!"

"Not funny."

"Nah, it is. Live a little, dude! Let the police handle the crime-fighting tonight. You've earned a night off."

Zach gestures to his bruised face. "Not if the Umbra Clan is capable of doing this. I won't rest."

Josh's eyes go wide. "No way Umbra did that kind of damage to you. No way! I refuse to believe it!"

"They were being controlled by something, some sort of energy. It made them much more powerful, and it gave them enhanced abilities." Zach narrows his eyes. "I was unprepared and outmatched, but I won't let it happen again."

Josh nods. "Oh no, I've seen that look before. Alright. Well..." He glances around, as if gathering his thoughts before looking Zach squarely in the eye. "Okay. What's the plan?"

"Uh... what do you mean, what's the plan? Aren't you hanging out with Brittney?"

"Well, yeah. But I can also help you, right?" He smirks at Zach's bloody face. "You definitely look like you need it."

"Not if you're bringing an innocent girl!"

"Aw, come on! It'll be fun! Just like the good old days!"

"The good old days were almost the death of me, Josh."

"No, the Umbra Clan was almost the death of you. Just look at your face!"

Zach rolls his eyes. "Fine. But if you bring the girl, I won't be responsible. Gear up, and let's move."

[ten minutes later]

"Ummm... Zach? I forgot my quiver. All I have is this one arrow."

Zach looks disdainfully at Josh as he holds a single arrow in his hands. "You can't be serious."

"Yeah, well I didn't think I'd be doing any superhero-ing any time soon, so I dumped the arrows out and used it to hold my golf clubs. It... didn't really work too well, though..."

Zach shakes his head. "Well, if you have only one shot, make it count."

"This is fun!" a girl calls out from behind them. "This is what you guys used to do back in your superhero days?"

"Sweetheart, every day is a superhero day for us!" Josh calls back, and the girl giggles.

Zach palms his forehead. "Focus, Josh. This could be a serious threat."

"All focused."

The two heroes approach the end of the rooftop and look down. Beneath them, a truck, being loaded up with crates by a group of cloaked figures, is quietly humming in the shadows. Zach gestures to Brittney to stay quiet and nods to Josh.

"This is them," he says in a low voice. He grabs his binoculars and zooms in on the truck so he can analyze the operation below. Every thug is moving purposefully, loading up the truck without saying a single word. However, some of them seem different. Quicker, sharper, and with almost robotic-like movements. Zach's eyes narrow.

"The Cyber Gang are here and working with Umbra. But why?"

Josh nods his understanding. The Cyber Gang has always caused trouble for the Protectors. A clan of cybernetic criminals who install advanced technology into their bodies, giving them enhanced abilities and hacking powers, they are quick, cunning, and deadly. The gang leader, Victor Cyberian, has had many run-ins with the Protectors before and is one of the most feared criminals in the city. Zach grits his teeth as he spots Victor standing near the truck, silently overseeing the operation.

"Interesting," Zach says. "The Umbra Clan is following Victor Cyberian's orders. I wonder why."

Josh grins. "What is even more interesting is deciding who on that street is going to get hit by this arrow." He holds up his single arrow for Brittney to see. "What do you think, Brit?"

The girl giggles. "The bad guy!" she says about nobody in particular.

"Okay, here's the plan," Zach says. "I'll go in unnoticed and cause a distraction, leading them away from the truck. Then you..." He glances up to see that Josh is nowhere to be found.

"WHAT'S UP, LOSERS!" Josh yells, jumping off the building and firing his arrow at Victor Cyberian. The advanced cyborg instantly recognizes the danger and dodges the arrow, causing it to slam into a canister behind him.

"The greatest archer in the world, and his only arrow doesn't hit his target..." Zach mutters to himself, before springing into action. He dives down into the alleyway, using his combat neo-suit to noiselessly scale the wall. Then, he grabs his electric shock baton and silently electrocutes the two Umbra guards standing watch, unaware of his presence.

"Ah, crud," Zach hears Josh say. He glances up to see his brother surrounded by a group of Umbra and Cyberclan thugs, with just a useless bow in his hands.

"Just kidding!" Josh cries as the canister leaks, showering the area in steam and blinding the Umbra guards. Zach moves quickly forward, using the distraction to take out two more

Umbra Clan thugs, but then he is knocked backward by a cyber-netic punch. A Cyber Gang thug, seemingly unaffected by the blinding steam, stands over him. The thug launches at Zach with his rocket-powered fist, missing his head by an inch, and then grabs a plasma blade and hurls it at the grizzled Protector, hoping to take him down in one swift blow.

Unfortunately for this cybernetic soldier, he has no idea who he is dealing with. Zach catches the plasma blade in midair and hurls it back at the cybergang thug with twice the power! Before the thug can react, the blade slices through his life support relay, causing him to crumble to the ground.

Zach looks around as the steam begins to clear and notices his brother fighting an Umbra Clan crook. Renowned instead for his deadly accuracy from long distances, Josh has never been an expert in hand-to-hand combat, and this fight is proving it. The Umbra Clan thug's punches are powerful, more powerful than any mortal man should ever be capable of, and Josh is losing ground.

"Interesting..." Zach says to himself, as the Umbra guard punches a road sign in half. "What could be giving these Umbra guys all of this power?"

"Uh, Zach? A little help?" Josh shouts.

One more punch and he could be defeated!

"AAAAGH!" The Umbra Clan thug screams in pain as Zach zaps the back of his head with his electric batons. He falls, unconscious, to the ground.

"I had him!" Josh exclaims.

"Yeah, right." Zach picks up Josh's arrow, which has been laying on the ground since the canister exploded. He glances up as the remaining two Cybergang thugs flee down the alleyway. "So much for questioning the enemy." Zach sighs. "Let's go see what was in that truck."

The two heroes turn and walk toward the vehicle, surveying the aftermath of the battle in front of them. This operation was previously planned and well organized. With Umbra Clan and the Cyber Gang working together, there must be something the heroes are missing.

"How did the Umbra Clan get the Cyber Gang to work with them?" Josh asks, as the pair approach the truck. "I thought they hated each other."

"I did too," Zach responds. "There must be something very profitable, or very dangerous, on the line. Especially if Victor Cyberian himself is overseeing the operation."

"Yeah. I didn't see him once the battle started, by the way. He must have fled while we were fighting."

Zach nods. "Typical Victor. But he will be back. He always is."

The two veteran heroes climb onto the truck and walk over to the wooden crates, stacked neatly along the wall. Then, in one fluid motion, Zach grabs his baton and smashes one of the crates. Immediately, both heroes look inside and gasp in surprise. Staring back at them is a glowing block of darkness and power. Emanating a void of evil and an aura of bloodthirst, the block seems to consume the light from the rest of the truck, shrouding its surroundings in sorrow.

And power, immense power.

Zach and Josh glance at each other, each understanding the gravity of the situation.

"This is a problem," Josh says.

Zach nods. "Yes. The Apex Imperium has returned."

7

EDUCATION

[staring intensely at Zach's french fries]
Josh

What? Do you want one?
Zach

No... [staring continues]
Josh

83

What?!
Josh

*Don't worry, it's just a
Game of Thrones reference...*
Zach

WHEN ZACH WAS IN ELEMENTARY SCHOOL, HE
struggled to succeed.

Public schools are generally limited in what they can offer students, due to regulations and, of course, funding. In most schools, there are regular, mainstream classes in which the majority of students can find success. Typical elementary school teachers instruct multiple subjects, perform basic lessons, assign homework, and evaluate their students with quizzes and tests. Most kids will progress through these classes without a problem throughout middle school and beyond. For the more advanced students, accelerated programs usually exist to further enhance and challenge their education, and for students in need of learning support, special classes are often taught separately and at a modified pace. For students on the autistic spectrum, learning aides are sometimes available to help the students individually succeed. However, the degree of their training can vary greatly.

At first glance, it seems like most public schools, with grants and other funding, have their bases covered. But for *our* local elementary school, Zach seemed to be a challenge. Here came a kid who claimed to be incredibly advanced in reading but incredibly behind in math, writing, phonetics, problem-solving, auditory and visual processing, and speech. A kid whose autistic symptoms were just severe enough to be detrimental to his learning experience in the classroom, but not severe enough for the learning aides to understand how to help him. A kid who was trying so hard to succeed but was constantly held back by basic fundamentals that he simply didn't understand. A kid who was constantly doubted and underestimated simply because his brain worked differently than everybody else's. For the record, this kid was in no way a behavior problem or a distraction to his classmates. His frustration played out in his tendency to retreat into a book. He didn't require extra attention to moderate his behavior. He only needed someone to understand that his way of learning was not necessarily addressed in the standard way of teaching used in the classroom.

What did the local elementary school do to help this kid? In 2006, they put Zach in learning support classes and hoped that their "problem" would go away. The classes didn't change how Zach was taught. They only taught him the state-mandated curriculum at a much slower pace than the mainstream classes. These were classes for kids who didn't know how to read and kids who required step-by-step instructions to combine letters and sounds to phonetically sound out words. But Zach's world revolved around reading. He had figured out how to do it in his own way, and the truth was, these fundamentals just weren't appropriate for his learning style.

Naturally, my parents fought tooth and nail for my brother, meeting with teachers, the school psychologist, and the principal. They sent countless emails, brought in outside doctors and advocates, quoted government standards, threatened legal action on multiple occasions, and did everything they could to give Zach the education he deserved. But the school wanted no business with my brother or my parents.

———

To: *************

From: Cheryl and Eric Stehle
Date: 3/2/2007

...However, after observing the curriculum, we quickly realized that while this program is appropriate for some students with learning disabilities, it is not the appropriate educational setting for Zach.

The lesson we observed was based on several predictable phonetic patterns and addressed phonetic awareness. However, Zach's advanced reading level and extensive sight recognition of words would make this lesson futile for him. In a class structured to address the needs of children with weak to grade-level reading skills, Zach's advanced reading and comprehension level could not be accommodated. This class addresses specific skills and not the learning disability that affects Zach's overall ability to perform.

Rather than focusing on his weaknesses (e.g., phonemic awareness), we appeal to the school district to recognize and capitalize on his strengths. Zach is a child who learns differently. He is not a child that does not learn. We strongly feel that an appropriate educational experience cannot be attained by fitting him into this type of learning support program.

...this letter serves as a written notice that we disapprove of placing Zach in the Learning Support for Language Arts. We now place the responsibility on the school to find a way to address his unique needs as required by U.S. Federal and Pennsylvania state laws which clearly state that the education and placement must be fitted to the child, not the child to a pre-packaged program which does not address his needs.

Please reference 20 U.S.C 1412 (5)(B) which provides that states must have in place procedures assuring that "children with disabilities, including children... are educated with children who are not disabled." This is implemented by 34 CFR 300-500 - 300-556.

Please also reference the Individuals with Disabilities Act (IDEA) which clearly states that a lack of adequate personnel or resources does not relieve school districts of the obligations to make free appropriate public education (FAPE) available to each disabled student in the least restrictive educational (LRE) setting.

Signed,
Cheryl and Eric Stehle

After much angst and frustration, Zach transferred schools in fifth grade.

Finding a school environment that fit Zach's unique educational needs proved difficult. He required a system that could prioritize how he learned and teachers who would engage with his strengths while simultaneously working on his weaknesses in a way that he could understand. To begin middle school, Zach transferred to a small private school specifically for kids who learned differently. The move was great at first, but the school's low enrollment and financial needs caused the admissions department to open their doors to an expanded student demographic. By seventh grade, Zach's school was primarily focused on students who were "forced out" of their former institutions due to behavior problems rather than students who had learning differences. For my innocent brother, the school became a nightmare from which he would come home telling stories of kids threatening to blow up the building. Teachers became more consumed with behavioral management than with individual learning plans, and the school was rapidly losing its mission to support learners with different learning styles. Before the year had ended, my parents knew that Zach's school environment needed to change yet again. He was stressed by the behavior of the other kids, becoming even more withdrawn from any social interaction outside of the family. He was obviously not getting the academic attention he had been receiving the previous school year.

Many years later, after Zach had moved on from this middle school, the principal was arrested for molesting several male students. This was the same principal who had previously tutored Zach when he was in sixth grade and had even been invited to Zach's Bar Mitzvah. Zach has never expressed a personal connection to this conduct, and we remain hopeful that we didn't miss anything.

Fortunately, by the end of seventh grade, my parents had found a new school for Zach. A cyber school with an on-site location close to home, this educational environment was able to address Zach's unique needs while providing him with quality instruction. The school had a wide array of teachers who specialized in online teaching (before it became cool in 2020... thanks, COVID-19...), and it offered the same standard, accelerated, and AP level classes found at most public high schools. Although Zach's new school did require my mother (a former teacher herself) to be his primary academic support, it also offered him on-site speech therapy and the availability of an assigned special education liaison. The one missing component of this new opportunity for Zach was social interaction. Zach had his books, though, so he didn't seem to care. Regardless, my mother managed to do some networking with some other parents from the school, and through these efforts, Zach met another local student who he still calls one of his best friends to this day. See number seven on the Protectors list!

After taking multiple AP-level reading and history classes, taking college prep courses, and studying incredibly hard, **Zach graduated from high school with a 4.4 GPA.**

He then progressed to the local community college, where he took every available history class because he loves reading stories! Three years later, he received an associate degree in Applied Sciences.

Honestly, it should have been a history degree, but accomplishing that required two semesters of language study. That was not exactly an endeavor for my brother, who continues to struggle with basic English diction.

That's okay. Zach doesn't need some degree to prove that he is amazing. That's why he has me.

THE "R" WORD

Has anyone ever said the word "retard" to you?
Josh

[shrugs] I don't usually pay attention to stuff like that.
Zach

Good. People who say that word don't deserve your attention anyway.
Josh

EVERYBODY HAS THOSE MOMENTS. YOU'RE

going about your normal day when, suddenly, you forget something incredibly basic. Of course, you refuse to Google it because that would be insulting to your own intelligence. Whatever you cannot remember, whether it be the title of some book you are reading, how to spell the word "pencil," or even just the name of your dog, you insist on racking your brain until you think of it.

Well, at least I hope that happens to everybody, or I've got a serious problem on my hands. Anyway, I had one of those moments earlier today. I was thinking about the origin of the "R" word, and I distinctly remembered that the word has a Latin root. I was also incredibly aware that I had taken six years of Latin classes from seventh grade to twelfth grade and, therefore, was as prepared as anyone to solve this dilemma without the use of Google!

Then, after two minutes of remembering almost nothing about Latin, I decided to Google it! (Blame my Latin teacher, not me. Sorry, Magistra!)

The word, *retard* comes from the Latin verb, *retardāre*, which means to hinder or make slow. My Latin teacher should be proud of me because I knew that *retardāre* is an infinitive verb and, therefore, had an "āre" ending. What I didn't know was how such an innocent word has gained such a negative and hurtful connotation over the past few decades.

The word, *retard* didn't begin its infiltration into the English language until, well, the English. As the British Empire grew, the word was adopted and used similarly to words such as "slow" or "delay." It wasn't until 1704 that the word was first printed in an American newspaper, and it wasn't until the 1960s that it began to mean anything more than its dead Latin roots. This is when things began to get interesting. Around the time of the Cuban Missile Crisis, the first-ever Super Bowl, and even the debut of Sesame Street, the label of "mental retardation" began to be pushed among disability activists as a replacement for terms such as "moron," "imbecile," and "idiot," as they believed that those words had all developed negative connotations. The use of the word *retard* began to spread throughout the 1970s. By the 1980s, it was widely accepted to call those with a cognitive disorder "mentally retarded" or, simply, a "retard." What began as an honest attempt to shift the notions surrounding mental disabilities culminated in the contamination of the word *retard*, giving the word the negative connotation we know today.

What does the "R" word mean today? It is an insult. It is hate speech. It is a slur. The "R" word refers to any form of the word *retard* or the ending "-tard" and embodies hatred toward any person with a mental disability.

Therefore, it is our job to correct those who say the "R" word. It is our duty as a community to speak up against this disgusting word and eliminate it from our language. In 2010, President Barack Obama signed "Rosa's Law," which mandated that all mention of "mental retardation" shall be referred to as "intellectual disability" in U.S. federal law. This change was inspired by a nine-year-old girl with Down Syndrome named Rosa Marcellino, and it has been an important milestone in the promotion of inclusion in the U.S government.

However, one president's signature isn't enough. To truly abolish this hateful word, it will take a community effort. Speaking up just once will not be enough, and just one person cannot make enough of a difference. **If we want to eradicate the "R" word, we must all make our voices heard, and our voices must never go away.**

Our voices cannot falter because it is so easy to have those moments, those times when you're going about your normal day, and, suddenly, you forget. Somebody says the word *retard,* and you don't speak up. You don't explain to them that the word is a slur, it is hateful, and it is wrong. You don't describe what the word means to somebody with an intellectual disability, and you don't request that they use a different word.

And then the moment is gone, and we're back where we started.

9

THE NICEST PERSON ON EARTH

Josh, you are the greatest chef in the entire world!
Zach

Even better than Gordon Ramsay?
Josh

Yep!
Zach

ONE DAY, ZACH AND I WERE WAITING IN LINE AT Five Guys.

It was a Thursday night, and the restaurant was packed. As two overwhelmed employees dashed between the grill and the register, trying in vain to keep pace with the growing number of orders, Zach and I waited patiently for our food. Each time a number was called, every person in the place looked down at their receipt, groaned when it wasn't their order, and then watched in envy as that lucky customer scooped up their greasy brown bags and walked out of the store, happy to finally receive their meal. This dynamic seemed to have been going on long before Zach and I had arrived that evening, and after thirty-five minutes of waiting we both knew that we weren't going to receive our food any time soon.

"Order 68!" The worker's voice cracked harshly as he shouted the number. Perhaps it was from stress. Not only were new burger orders coming in each minute, but the kid also had to deal with angry customers coming up to him and demanding to know what was taking so long. In the time that Zach and I had been in the restaurant, this had happened on two separate occasions. However, the look on the kid's face told me that he had been dealing with it all night long. The kid gulped quickly before turning and rushing over to the fry station, nearly tripping on the wet floor in the process.

"Dang kid…" a man muttered next to me. He, like everybody in the restaurant, had apparently been waiting the entire night for his food. He turned to me. "Can always count on this place to keep you waiting. And then *this* is the product." He gestured over to the burgers that had turned into meat slabs of all different shapes and sizes because the only other employee who was manning the grill was swamped so badly with orders that he couldn't keep up.

I remember nodding. I admit it.

For the thirty-five minutes Zach and I had spent waiting for our burgers, on that day, the food did not look very appetizing.

Then Zach looked up from his phone. He had been reading a virtual comic book, seemingly oblivious to the mayhem of the restaurant around him. He took one glance at the workers and said, "I hope those workers have a good day off tomorrow. This looks really hectic."

Then, without another word, Zach returned to his comic book.

About ten minutes later, our order number was called.

I was hungry. Zach was hungry. But it has always been a Zach Stehle rule that Five Guys food is only to be eaten at the kitchen table at home, and not at the restaurant. So, I grabbed our greasy brown bag and headed for the door, eager to reach our final destination as quickly as possible and dig in. Then, just as we approached the door, we noticed chaos in the making.

Two Five Guys employees were on the other side, struggling to move a massive, heavy wooden box through the entrance. They were moving quite slowly (their long day had definitely taken its toll), and their dolly's wheels were both helplessly broken, leaving them stranded with a giant heavy box right inside the first door. Around the two men, a few people stood by and stared, but it seemed that nobody had offered to help.

Two distinct thoughts ran through my mind at that moment.

My first instinct was to move past the men quickly so we could make it outside before they completely blocked the entrance and left us trapped inside. After all, Zach and I hadn't eaten all day, and the box moving process in front of us looked like it was about to be a very long ordeal. But other people were waiting by the door, thinking similarly to me, obstructing our way forward. I paused at the front of the door.

Then, I came up with an even better idea.

"Hey, Zach," I said. "Why don't we eat inside today, while the food is still hot? These guys are going to block the exit out—"

"Ah!" Zach interrupted me. He scurried through the first door and grabbed the second one firmly, holding it open for the two employees. The employee closest to my brother nodded his thanks and wiped the sweat from his forehead.

I glanced back down at the greasy brown bag in my hands. Had thirty-five minutes of waiting for this food made me above helping these men carry this box? It was my first instinct to get by, but it was Zach's first instinct to help.

I placed the brown bag on a nearby table and approached the door, looking for a way to assist the two men, but I was too late. A few other people had seen Zach's eagerness to help out and had followed suit, leaving me with little opportunity to contribute.

THE NICEST PERSON ON EARTH

I stood and watched Zach hold that door open with a smile on his face for ten minutes, as the team of Five Guys employees and random people half-carried and half-shoved that massive box through the door.

Then Zach looked over at me, a confused look on his face. "Well, what are we waiting for? I'm hungry. Let's go!"

Several days later, I was driving to the post office.

Usually, when I drive, I like to listen to music. I sometimes even sing (badly) when I'm in the mood. But that day, my ride was silent. Usually, when I drive, I like to sit back and roll down the windows to smell the air. But that day, I was sitting up straight, and my eyes were locked on the road. I was not in a good mood.

My day had begun like any other: with the simple errand of driving to the post office to drop off a few bills that I promised my parents I would mail for them. It was only after I arrived that I realized I had forgotten the stack of envelopes at home, and now I had to drive all the way back to get them. So, I turned back onto the highway and drove home, wasting an extra forty minutes in the process due to sitting in miles of standstill traffic. Then, as I pulled into my driveway, I remembered that I had planned to meet my friend for lunch that day and that he wanted to get food at a new restaurant right next to that very same post office. So, I got back into my car for a second time and drove that tedious forty minutes back to the post office. Once the building was in sight, I called my friend. I was ready for our meal, at last.

1. He canceled on me.

2. I realized I had forgotten the envelopes for a second time.

3. I realized I also had to go to the bank.

4. It was raining outside, and my ankle was sprained.

Now you're all caught up! I was having a bad day. Just when things didn't seem like they could get any worse, somebody drove right through a stop sign and nearly hit me with his car. When I looked through the car window and saw that the driver was staring at his phone, I nearly lost my mind. If he had been driving just a foot closer to me, I could have been seriously hurt.

I pulled over to the side of the road and slammed on my car horn, angry at how my day was going.

After gaining my composure, I drove to the bank and found a parking spot that was barely big enough for my car because the owner of a large truck decided to use more than his fair share of the outlined space. I flipped my hoodie over my head and trudged toward the entrance. By the door, a teenage-ish girl stood over an eave and rang a bell over a Salvation Army bucket. She smiled as a man walked out of the bank. She looked up at him and asked him for a donation, but the man just laughed and walked off. So, she turned to me.

"Hi, there! And what's your name, my friend?"

I raised an eyebrow. "I'm Josh."

"Hi, Josh! My name's Stacey. I'm here with the Salvation Army! We're looking to help those in our community who cannot afford necessities such as utilities, food, and water. Would you like to donate to help our cause?"

I recall this moment vividly. Remember, I was having a bad day. Honestly, if there was ever a time in which I felt justified in saying "no, thank you, not today," it was in this moment. If fact, if there was ever a time in which it was justified for me to say, "I'd rather shipwreck off the coast of Lian Yu than donate today, thank you," it was also this moment. (Yep, that's a Green Arrow reference.)

To be completely honest, I can't remember a single time before that day in which I donated to the Salvation Army. It's not that I didn't believe in the cause or the organization, and it also wasn't because I was too selfish to care. Over the years, I had performed many other aspects of giving very actively. I was an outspoken volunteer for multiple autism awareness organizations and events, and I donated regularly to multiple autism foundations and charities.

However, when it came to being approached on the street and being asked to give money, I had simply developed an automatic response, "no, thank you." I think that many people can relate to this. To me, my refusal to pay a little more, or "round up my total to the nearest dollar" was not out of a place of ill intent. I simply believed I had no way of trusting the people (or companies) taking my money. Were they truly going to provide this extra dollar to people in need or just pocket the cash themselves? What percentage of my money was actually going to the cause they were advertising? So, I opened my mouth, prepared to say, "not today, thanks."

But instead, my mind jumped to this thought:

What would Zach say?

Because unlike me, Zach hadn't questioned the quality of the food at the Five Guys that day. He simply trusted that the workers behind the grill had his best intentions in mind and were doing everything they could to make him the best burger possible. When we left the restaurant, Zach didn't worry if the workers would react negatively to him when he tried to help them move their boxes. He simply acted through the goodness of his heart.

And even if my brother were to experience all of the unfortunate events that had happened throughout my day, I know that he would never refuse the basic and selfless act of giving to a charity.

At that moment, I realized that, during all times I *questioned* the sincerity of people, Zach *assumed* they were all decent people like him just trying to do good in the world.

This is simply who my brother is. He's always searching for ways to make the people around him happier. Even if it seems too insignificant or bothersome for most people, Zach always strives to help. Of course, they aren't always the grandest of gestures. For example, Zach has never bought me a new car, and he'll probably never take me on a trip to Paris. (You should though, dude.) But what he lacks in flair, he makes up for in compassion, selflessness, and utter kindness. Zach brings home flowers for my mom or donut holes for me when he gets off work. He holds doors open for others, donates money to trustworthy causes (and some untrustworthy ones too), and randomly compliments friends, family, and complete strangers. He expresses his love freely, his admiration profusely, and his appreciation abundantly. Zach wakes up every day and tries to make the lives of the people around him better. Regardless of what he may be feeling that day, my brother strives to make the world a better place.

So, I turned back to Stacey, and despite the bad day I was having, I said,

"Sure. Here's a nickel."

Just kidding. I didn't reenact Zach's encounter with Snapback Dude because I had more money in my wallet than five cents. I had a $5 bill and two $1s, to be exact. I gave all $7.00 to Stacey. I know it wasn't a huge donation. What's $7.00, after all? But for me, it was a life-changing experience because, despite the day I was having and in spite of my previous reactions to people asking for money, I stepped outside myself and became Zach-like. And it felt really, really good. I had taken one step closer to being more like my big brother and best friend.

This is the effect Zach has on people. This is his superpower.

10

I AM A SUPERHERO EXPERT

You're my best friend.
Zach

No, you're my best friend.
Josh

No, you're my best friend.
Zach

Right. Isn't that how it works?
Josh

Yep. See? I win!
Zach

I AM A SUPERHERO EXPERT.

This is somewhat deceiving to say, considering I know almost nothing about superheroes, at least when compared to an actual expert.

Sure, I understand the basics. I've read plenty of comic books since my childhood, and I've seen almost all the superhero movies. But unlike my best friend, Zach, I don't completely understand the intricacies of the Marvel Cinematic Universe, and I've never memorized the DC Universe storylines and their many villains. And, sadly, I probably couldn't name the original seven members of the Justice League, even if Batman held me by my ankles off the side of a building. In fact, after writing this book, I realize that I confuse a heck of a lot more superheroes than just the members of the Justice League.

Nevertheless, I do consider myself a superhero expert.

I'm an expert in many other things, too. I have learned how to look out for troublesome beggars on the side of the road. I have mastered the art of losing "Death Battle" predictions, even though I should have a 50/50 chance at each episode. I have become a seasoned superhero author myself, though not without the guidance of my very own comic book master, Zach Stehle.

I have learned how to listen. My brother may be a quiet, soft-spoken man, but his mind is bright and imaginative. Like so many people with autism, Zach has so much to offer the world. He just needs to be given the chance.

I have learned how to learn. Everybody faces challenges, and everybody's challenges are unique to themselves. Watching my brother overcome his obstacles and grow into the man he is today fills me with pride and teaches me the values of hard work, humility, kindness, and integrity. My brother has shown me how to be good, how to be strong, and how to persevere. He's constantly searching for ways to make people smile, and he's always ready to lend a hand to those in need. I try to learn from him every day. He's the best teacher.

Zach emulates his favorite superheroes in everything he does. He lives by their words of courage and hope, and he replicates their acts of generosity and selflessness. Zach is the nicest person on the planet Earth and tries every day to make the world a better place.

I, too, emulate my favorite superhero.

Zach is my superhero; therefore, as I have attested,

I am a superhero expert.

THANK YOU!

HI! THIS IS ZACH STEHLE, AND I WANT TO THANK
you guys for reading *I am a Superhero Expert*. Josh, the author of
this book and my brother, worked really hard on this. I hope you
guys enjoy it and leave it with a new understanding of autism
like I did.

As Josh states in the book, I am autistic, and it has been both
challenging and interesting in my life. Autism allows me to see
the world in a different light and gave birth to my imagination,
which has been a comfort to me in troubled times. It also gives
me something to do. Yet, autism has made it difficult for me
to speak properly to other people. It is also hard for me to pay
attention or even do things that seem easy.

Sometimes, I hate the fact I am autistic, and I desire to be
normal. Yet, I get through it with help from my family who have
been my biggest supporters. They fight for me, help me, and are
always there to offer comfort, advice, and assistance. They have
always shown me that autism is not something to be ashamed
of; it is just part of who I am.

Josh, especially, is my biggest supporter of this. He always listens to my ideas and my stories. He gives me advice and is always
there for me when I need it. For this, I am eternally grateful. Josh
is more than my brother; he is my best friend and partner. I try
my best to show interest in his interests. Fortunately, because
we share many of the same interests, it makes it easy for us to
retain common ground.

Going back to my feelings about autism, I see benefits from
having it. My vast imagination plays home to many stories and

characters, all based on or inspired by my favorite universes. My ability to quickly understand the lore and the history of fiction gives me the framework to build upon common features and expand upon them in my own ways. Just recently, Josh and I began writing a series of books based on my Imagination Universe. You read the first few pages in chapter six of this book. This is something that I wish we did sooner, given how much fun I am having. We are hoping to publish *The Protectors: Generations* soon. Stay tuned!

I hope this book leads to a greater understanding of people with autism. We are not different; we just have trouble and challenges in some areas of life and do better in other areas. That is common in life. We all do better in some areas. Some people are better at talking or doing physical activities than others, yet they might struggle in other areas like problem-solving. The important thing to remember is that we are all human, with our strengths, flaws, and issues. We should judge each other based on our character, not what is on the outside.

Thank you for reading *I am a Superhero Expert.*

Zach Stehle

ACKNOWLEDGMENTS

TO DR. JAMIE MOZZONE, MY LOVE FOR WRITING flourished in your 10th grade classroom. Before AP Language, I couldn't have been bothered to open a Word document unless my grade was on the line. Now, I do it during my free time. This book would not have been possible without the support and incredible instruction I received in your English classes. Thank you.

To Karl Jean-Baptiste, until I met you, I didn't believe I could be an author, but you never doubted me. You are the one who inspired me to go all in and chase this dream, and I am eternally grateful. Thank you.

To Valerie Shay, I had a lot of grand ideas, interesting curveballs, and a unique, particular vision for *I am a Superhero Expert*. Your guidance, knowledge, and expertise made capturing that vision possible. Your contributions to this book have been immeasurable. Thank you.

To Becca, Mom, and Dad, *I am a Superhero Expert* would not be possible without your never-ending support. I cannot express how appreciative I am of the time, effort, heart, and soul you have poured into helping Zach and me achieve our dreams. Thank you for the many sacrifices and commitments you have made. Thank you for the unconditional love. Thank you for always believing in me. Thank you.

And to Zach, well, what is left to be said? I guess, I'm sorry for exposing our little secret in Chapter 2, but I hope you can forgive me for that one. It makes for an entertaining story. The good news is that we are about to publish *The Protectors:*

Generations together, and I hope it is going to be a massive hit. Maybe even a best seller! But anyway, I love you, Zach. Thank you for everything.

BOOK CLUB QUESTIONS

1. What is autism?

2. A single word used in casual conversation affects the author so deeply that it sets him off on a mission of discovery. Have you ever been affected by someone else's words or actions?

3. How would you change if somebody with special needs entered your life?

4. Treating somebody with dignity can be interpreted in many ways. What does it mean to you?

5. Would you recognize an autistic person? Why?

6. Would your behavior change if you knew somebody was autistic? Should it?

7. Should children be taught formally in school how to interact with people with disabilities? Should this be part of a formal curriculum?

8. Do you feel that educators should be required to learn how to teach neurodiverse students? If so, how should they be taught?

9. How important is it to make sure that people are aware of another person's diagnosis? Should they share it?

AUTHOR BIO

JOSH STEHLE IS AN AUTHOR, ADVOCATE, AND leader in the autism community. He grew up in Philadelphia, PA, with his older brother, Zach, and twin sister, Becca. In his free time, Josh enjoys attending autism awareness events, taking his brother to lunch, and spending time with his family. The two brothers have gained global attention for their autism awareness social media brand, "The Stehle Bros," receiving millions of views on TikTok and Instagram and being featured on ABC News, The Art of Autism, and more! Follow Josh Stehle on Instagram and Facebook at "joshstehle," and sign up for his newsletter today at *www.joshstehle.com*!

More books from 4 Horsemen Publications & Accomplishing Innovation Press

4HP Writer's Resources
The Author's Accountability Planner

The General Worldbuilding Guide
The Science Fiction
Worldbuilding Guide
The Paranormal Worldbuilding Guide
The Romance Worldbuilding Guide
The Fantasy Worldbuilding Guide

Jörgen Jensen with Peter Lundgren
Mind Over Tennis: Mastering the
Mental Game

Josh Stehle
I Am A Suphero Expert: Growing Up
with my Autistic Brother

Kiyomi Holland
HeARTwork

Lael Giebel
Sustainability is for Everyone: Beginning
Steps to Creating a Sustainability
Program for Your Business

Letitia Washington
The Psychology of Character Building
for Authors

Megan Mackie
Advanced Con Quest

N.B. Johnson
Wonders and Miracles

Valerie Willis
Writer's Bane: Research
Writer's Bane: Formatting 101
Writer's Bane: Plot & Foreshadowing
Writer's Bane: Revisions & Edition (w/
JM Paquette)
Writer's Bane: Character Development

Academia & Textbooks

Dr. Jenifer Paquette
Sentence Diagramming 101: Fun with
Linguistics (and Movies)

Textbooks
Composition and Grammar: For
HCC by HCC

Discover more at
4HorsemenPublications.com

CPSIA information can be obtained
at www.ICGtesting.com
Printed in the USA
BVHW041545200123
656705BV00013BA/72/J

9 798823 200264